RAMEN

NOODLE

COOKBOOK

RAMEN NOODLE COOKBOOK

Nell Benton

British Edition
Project Editor: Kathryn Meeker
Senior Art Editor: Glenda Fisher
Angliciser: Claire Cross
Managing Editor: Stephanie Farrow
Managing Art Editor: Christine Keilty
Pre-production Producers: Rebecca Fallowfield & Tony Phipps
Senior Producer: Stephanie McConnell

American Edition
Publisher: Mike Sanders
Associate Publisher: Billy Fields
Executive Acquisitions Editor: Nathalie Mornu
Cover and Book Designer: XAB Design
Photographer: Michael Berman
Food Stylist: Laura Kinsey-Dolph
Development Editor: Kayla Dugger
Compositor: Ayanna Lacey
Proofreader: Monica Stone
Indexer: Heather McNeill

First published in Great Britain in 2015 by
Dorling Kindersley Limited
80 Strand, London, WC2R 0RL

CONTENTS

iNTRODUCTiON TO RAMEN

What is the ramen obsession all about? This Japanese soul-food dish has been popping up all over the world as ramen enthusiasts re-create and build upon the traditional bowl of ramen. By knowing the history and techniques behind ramen, you can start to embrace this truly special dish.

A BACKGROUND ON RAMEN

Forget the highly salted packet noodles you subsisted on as a student, traditional ramen is made from fresh noodles, broth, and toppings. The finished result yields a simple, delicious, and beautiful bowl of ramen – and a labour of love, from start to finish.

1900
Ramen originally came from China, as a variation of a dish called *lamian*. There is a consensus that Chinese immigrants established ramen shops in Japan prior to World War II, but the exact date of its arrival is unknown.

1958
In 1958, Momofuku Ando invented instant ramen, which was sold in **little blocks wrapped in colourful plastic packaging**. They were made by frying cooked noodles briefly at a high heat, so they could later be rehydrated with hot water.

1985
The movie *Tampopo,* a Japanese comedy, tells the story of two lorry drivers who teach a ramen shop owner how to improve her fare. It contains scenes on how to eat ramen properly, as well as the love that must go into making the broth.

1945
After the war, many Japanese soldiers returned home from China with an appreciation for lamian, and some quickly established **restaurants with ramen on the menu**. Ramen's popularity quickly increased.

1971
Taking his creation one step further, in 1971, Momofuku Ando invented the **heat-resistant instant noodle cup** made of polystyrene. This allowed the noodles to be rehydrated without ever taking them out of the package.

1999
The Momofuku Ando Instant Ramen Museum opens in Osaka, Japan. It features a replica of the garden shed in which Ando developed instant ramen and hands-on exhibits that allow visitors to make their own noodles.

2008
Ramen Girl, an American-made film, focuses on an American girl living in Japan who learns about the art of making ramen, as well as the power of redemption contained in a well-made bowl of noodles.

2015-
Ramen chefs in Japan continue to create new and exciting variations based on ingredients available to them in this global market (known as *fusion*).

1994
The **Shin-Yokohama Raumen Museum** opens in Yokohama, Japan. Devoted to ramen soup, this food amusement park included branches of famous ramen restaurants from across Japan.

2004
Chef David Chang opens his first noodle restaurant, **Momofuku Noodle Bar, in New York City**. Its inventiveness with ingredients is arguably what started the ramen craze outside of Japan.

2011
CupNoodles Museum opens in Yokohama, Japan. It includes a room with more than 3,000 ramen product packages and a "factory" where visitors can embellish a foam cup and fill it with their choice of ingredients and toppings.

RAMEN ACROSS JAPAN

Just like different parts of Italy are known for their distinct dishes, and different regions of France for their wines, the same holds true for ramen in Japan. Ramen varies greatly from region to region, depending on climate, tradition, outside influence, and the availability of ingredients. While there are too many regional varieties of ramen to list, here are five regions that should be added to any ramen pilgrimage!

KYOTO

Kyoto is known for its chicken-based broth. Highly *kotteri*, or rich, the ramen broth is generally even thicker than tonkotsu and is served with a thin, straight noodle, usually softer than the average ramen noodle. Toppings can include garlic, kujnoegi onions, chives, and spicy bean paste.

HAKATA

Hakata is a ward in Fukuoka City, and there's general consensus that Fukuoka is the birthplace of tonkotsu, the wildly popular, milky-white, savory pork broth. This broth is created by boiling pork bones over a long period of time. To preserve the milky-white colour, the broth is usually seasoned with salt and/or miso. The noodles served are usually thin, firm, and straight. Typical toppings include chashu (braised pork), wood ear mushrooms, spring onions, and spicy mustard greens.

KYOTO

HAKATA

Seaside towns are more likely to use local fish and seafood in the broth and as toppings.

The cold north incorporates hearty miso into many of its broths.

SAPPORO

MURORAN

TOKYO

Eastern Japan generally favours lighter broths (*assari*).

SAPPORO

This city is famous for being the birthplace of miso ramen. Hearty, rich, fatty, and delicious, Sapporo ramen is *kotteri*. A classic Sapporo miso ramen is a pork and red miso-based broth, with minced pork, garlic, ginger, and sweetcorn that's then topped with a dollop of butter. The noodles served in Sapporo are typically thick and chewy.

MURORAN

Muroran is a northern port city known for its pork curry ramen. In Japan, curry is often associated with sailors, and so Muroran combined its traditional curry with the emerging ramen trend in the first half of the twentieth century. The broth resembles more of a thick curry sauce than a thin soup.

TOKYO

Tokyo-style ramen is typically a lighter broth (*assari*) most closely related to the original Chinese broth. Made with a hybrid of chicken and dashi fish stock with a soy sauce (*shoyu*) base, there are layers of flavour in this comforting dish. The style of noodle usually features medium-wide, curly noodles. Typical toppings include roast pork, spring onions, and bamboo shoots.

UMAMİ'S ROLE İN RAMEN

Umami is a Japanese word that translates roughly as "pleasant savoury taste", and it is defined as the fifth taste or flavour. Umami has been described as a rich, meaty, savoury taste that plays a significant role in making foods taste delicious and well-rounded.

THE HİSTORY BEHİND UMAMİ

The primary taste sensations – sweet, salty, sour, and bitter – are the base of flavour perceptions. Sweet and salty are easy to describe – think sugar and table salt. A good example of sour is lemon or lime. Bitter flavours include coffee and beer. However, umami is trickier to pin down.

Umami has as much to do with sensation as with flavour; along with its rich meatiness, it gives the impression of coating the tongue. It was first identified by Kikunae Ikeda in 1908 in kombu dashi. Around the same time, French chef Escoffier invented veal stock, which he found didn't fit in the four already existing taste sensations.

Asian cooking also relies heavily on balancing the four S's: sweet, salty, sour, and spicy. A perfect dish will be aesthetically pleasing and harmoniously flavoured.

Explaning taste
Umami is not only the fifth taste, but has also been described as the perfect combination of the four tastes.

- **SWEET** — Sugar
- Salted caramel
- Dark chocolate
- **SALTY** — Salt
- **UMAMI** — Veal stock
- **BITTER** — Coffee
- Margarita
- Pomegranate
- **SOUR** — Lime

North America: Bacon
Bacon provides a smoky, salty, and even a slightly sweet complement to dishes.

South America: Tomatoes
Raw or cooked, tomatoes provide a rich, sweet, and acidic flavour to dishes.

HOW RAMEN CAPTURES THE UMAMI FLAVOUR

Umami as a concept may have it's origins in Japan, but umami-rich foods have been eaten all over the world for centuries. Ramen combines umami-rich foods – whether Japanese, Western, or a mix of both – to create an especially flavoursome, balanced dish.

In Japan, umami-rich foods include kombu bonito flakes, fermented fish, fermented bean paste, soy sauce, green tea, and shiitake mushrooms. Kombu dashi stock is a great example of combining umami-rich ingredients that work well together.

In Western cuisine, umami foods include ham, asparagus, and aged cheese. These flavours describe a shared taste of rich fullness and meatiness. Another unlikely example of umami is tomatoes, which serve as the base of many sauces and condiments all over the world. The tomato miso ramen recipe is an example of a dish packed with Western umami-rich foods.

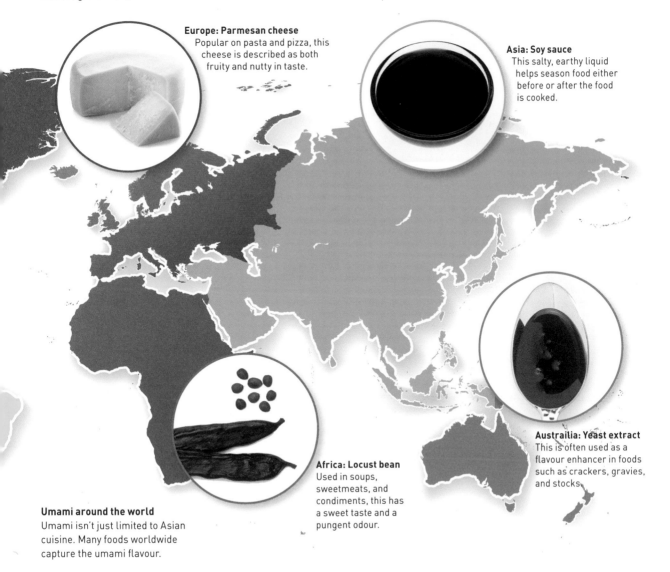

Europe: Parmesan cheese
Popular on pasta and pizza, this cheese is described as both fruity and nutty in taste.

Asia: Soy sauce
This salty, earthy liquid helps season food either before or after the food is cooked.

Africa: Locust bean
Used in soups, sweetmeats, and condiments, this has a sweet taste and a pungent odour.

Austrailia: Yeast extract
This is often used as a flavour enhancer in foods such as crackers, gravies, and stocks.

Umami around the world
Umami isn't just limited to Asian cuisine. Many foods worldwide capture the umami flavour.

WHAT iS FUSiON RAMEN?

In recent years, both Japanese and Western chefs have bucked tradition and created brash, bold takes on ramen. These contemporary twists of the classic recipes have brought about ramen fusion, where radical and traditional interpretations combine.

TRADiTiONAL

From 1641 to 1943, Japan had a policy of isolationism that prohibited most contact with foreigners. It had only limited relations with the Netherlands, China, Korea, and the Ryukyu Islands. This meant that up until World War II, Japanese cuisine had few outside influences. After the war, Japanese soldiers brought their favourite Chinese dishes, such as ramen, back to Japan and incorporated them into their own cuisine.

Flavours

Japanese cuisine has traditionally relied heavily on fish, rice, miso, noodles, and seasonal vegetables.

Ingredients

A typical ramen would be topped with items such as nori, soft-boiled eggs, menma, spring onions, and pork.

Presentation

Ramen has traditionally been served in large, deep bowls. The noodles, broth, toppings, and flourishes are all layered in the same bowl, then served piping hot to diners for greedy slurping.

Nori

Spring onions

Sweetcorn

Enoki mushrooms

FUSiON

Modern chefs have taken ramen to exciting new heights by playing with various aspects of the dish, incorporating their own favourite ingredients and culinary techniques.

Blended cuisines

Fusion ramen can include components as varied as taco beef from Mexico, curry pastes from Thailand, and North African harissa. Using ingredients from anywhere around the world, you can play with your favourites while maintaining harmony with the flavours and textures as in traditional ramen.

Novelty

Traditional Japanese flavours can be enhanced by the introduction of food items that were only recently brought to Japan, such as tomatoes, Brussels sprouts, and coconut milk.

Unexpected techniques

Modern chefs have introduced techniques from traditional French cooking, including torching, sous vide, and foams. Chefs trained in the French tradition have also contribute their knowledge of stocks to enhance ramen broths. Transforming packet ramen noodles into gnocchi is also one of the many ways chefs have used fun techniques to modernize ramen.

Modern plating

Ramen has evolved from being served in bowls to being served in a variety of ways. For instance, tsukemen – otherwise known as dipping ramen – is a deconstructed ramen where the broth, noodles, and toppings are served to diners separately.

Tomatoes

Brussels sprouts

Coconut milk

Parmesan

KiTCHEN EQUiPMENT

Having the proper kitchen equipment is very important in order to make the dishes in this book. However, don't feel you have to break the bank to stock up. Second-hand shops are a great place to source a lot of these items!

BOWLS

Mise en place bowls and plates Having multiple little bowls and plates to hold your prepared ingredients is the cleanest and most efficient way to set up your work station, allowing you to assemble your ramen bowl quickly.

Mixing bowls The two sizes of mixing bowls you need are a 1l (1¾ pint) mixing bowl for spices and smaller ingredients, and a 2.5l (4 pint) mixing bowl for larger ingredients.

CHOPPING AND CUTTING

Chef's knife Great for chopping, dicing, and slicing vegetables and meat. It usually has a 20–30.5cm (8–12in) blade and can come in a variety of sizes and weights. Simply choose a handle size and weight that's most comfortable for you.

Chopping boards These come in all shapes and sizes. It is best to use plastic chopping boards for meat, as they are easy to clean and sanitize. Wooden chopping boards can be used for vegetables.

Paring knife This smallish knife with a narrow-edge blade is perfect for more delicate kitchen work, such as peeling, skinning, and deveining your ingredients.

COOKiNG

Braising dish There are many different dishes that can be used to braise food – from casserole dishes, to cast-iron pots. As long as your ingredients fit with the lid snugly on, you can use whichever dish you prefer.

Lidded stockpot Having an 11.5l (20 pint) or larger stockpot in your kitchen is very handy for making large quantities of ramen stocks. Look for a stockpot that comes with a heavy lid.

Noodle basket Allows you to cook and strain noodles, as well as blanch small batches of vegetables.

Pots and pans From heating broth to searing pork belly chashu, having a variety of durable pots and pans is necessary. It's best to find pots and pans with lids; however, if you don't have lids for all of them, you can always use foil.

ROLLiNG

Rolling pin There's no shortage of choices when it comes to a pin for rolling out your noodle dough. Options of wooden, marble, and plastic can be found in a variety of shapes and sizes. Choose the rolling pin that feels the most comfortable for you.

Pasta roller and cutter An attachment can be fitted directly to a same-brand standing mixer. The roller and cutter roll out and portion the dough for noodles.

STRAiNiNG

Skimmer This is used to skim the scum that rises to the surface of a simmering broth. Fine-mesh skimmers are the best for this.

Fine-mesh strainer This is great for pouring liquid through to catch any small bits you don't want.

Colander Needed to rinse and clean the bones in ramen stocks. Colanders have larger holes than strainers, allowing the debris from bones to be easily discarded.

UTENSiLS

Ladle Great for portioning broth so you don't have to tilt a large pot. Choose a stainless-steel, sturdy ladle ideal for long-term use.

Slotted spoon Has holes or slots in the wide part of the spoon, allowing liquid to pass through while holding the food item. This is great for fishing out ingredients.

Tongs The ideal instrument for breaking up and portioning noodles, and for firmly grasping foods you're frying, grilling, or sautéing.

Rolling pin

An assortment of bowls

Noodle basket

Fine-mesh skimmer

Chef's knife

Chopping board

Fine-mesh strainer

SPOONS

Ramen spoons, also called Chinese duck spoons, are large spoons with short handles and high edges, to maximize the amount of broth you can hold in them. You can find the spoons made out of wood, ceramic, metal, and plastic.

CHOPSTICKS

Chopsticks help you retrieve and eat the noodles and toppings from the ramen bowl. They're made from a number of materials and come in a variety of sizes. Choose the size and type of chopsticks you're most comfortable using.

SERVING UTENSILS

Only three main serving utensils are needed for a standard bowl of ramen: bowls, spoons, and chopsticks. For specialty ramen, however, you may need some other serving dishes.

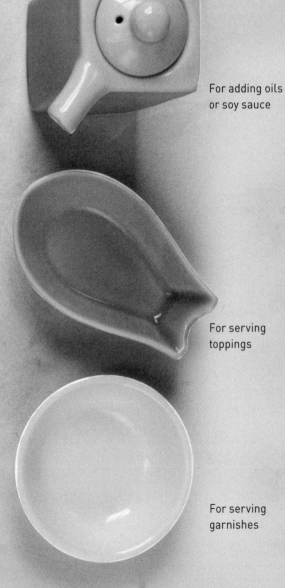

For adding oils
or soy sauce

For serving
toppings

For serving
garnishes

BOWLS

Large, deep bowls are preferable
for ramen, as you need a vessel big
enough to hold the broth, noodles, and
all of the toppings. Clay bowls work
the best because they retain heat, but
you can also use bowls made of
ceramic or plastic.

SERVING DISHES

For specialty ramen such as tsukemen,
or "dipping ramen", you'll need a variety
of serving dishes to accommodate the
broth, noodles, and toppings. For the
noodles you can use either a bamboo
mat, or any other vessel you have on
hand, such as a plate or a bowl.

HOW TO EAT RAMEN

When it comes to eating ramen, you're expected to eat quickly, slurp loudly, and finish all the noodles and toppings in the bowl. In Japan, if you finish all the noodles in your bowl before finishing the rest of the dish, you can order another serving.

HOLDING THE UTENSILS PROPERLY

You need just two utensils to eat ramen: chopsticks and a deep spoon.

- Chopsticks are held in your right hand and used to grab the solids in the bowl, such as the noodles.
- The deep spoon is held in your left hand and used to sip the broth.

Intersperse eating the noodles and sipping the broth.

Digging in right away

If you order a bowl of ramen in Japan, it will arrive scalding hot. It's expected that you eat it as fast as possible to avoid the noodles becoming mushy. At home, in order to serve it as hot as possible, be sure to have all of the ingredients ready so that you can assemble the bowl before any ingredients overcook.

Slurping the noodles

When eating the steaming hot ramen quickly, it's important to slurp your noodles. This cools them off just enough so that you don't burn your mouth.

HOW TO USE CHOPSTICKS

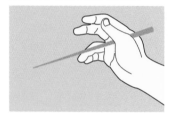

Rest one chopstick between the crook of your thumb and the top joint of your ring finger.

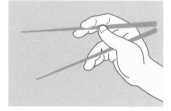

Place the other chopstick above it, holding it between your thumb and index finger.

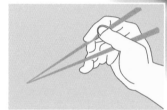

Practice moving the top chopstick up and down while keeping the lower one still.

GETTiNG TO THE BOTTOM OF RAMEN

Ramen, by definition, is a dish comprised of noodles, broth, and toppings. Understanding these components and how they work in harmony with each other is the first step in building the perfect bowl of ramen.

USiNG YOUR NOODLE

There's no standard ramen noodle. They can come in a variety of shapes and sizes, although most are made from high-gluten flour, salt, kansui water, and sometimes eggs. They are typically pale yellow in colour, firm, and chewy. Different noodles are used for different broths, depending on what style of ramen it is.

FRESH, FROZEN, DRY, OR iNSTANT?

Hardly anyone making ramen at home in Japan makes their own noodles, because good-quality, commercial ramen noodles are readily available. While you can buy frozen noodles in some shops, buying fresh is preferable. Fresh noodles can be found in a number of Japanese and Asian grocery stores in the refrigerated section, as well as some large supermarkets.

Instant ramen noodles are made by deep frying partially cooked noodles to dehydrate them into blocks. However, you can spend a bit more on instant noodles that have been partially cooked and air-dried, to avoid the deep-frying and the fat.

NARROW, WiDE, STRAiGHT, OR CURLY?

Sometimes, you'll see thinner, straight ramen noodles paired with a tonkotsu broth, and curly with a miso-based broth. Wide noodles are usually paired with a flavoursome broth to balance the natural taste of the noodle. If you're looking for curly noodles, these are achieved with special equipment. Winner Foods, based in London, UK, manufactures custom ramen noodles and gives an overview of the process on their website.

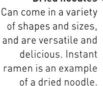

Fresh noodles
Comprised of strong flour, kansui, salt, and sometimes egg. Making your own fresh noodles is incredibly rewarding!

Dried noodles
Can come in a variety of shapes and sizes, and are versatile and delicious. Instant ramen is an example of a dried noodle.

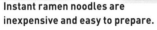
Instant ramen noodles are inexpensive and easy to prepare.

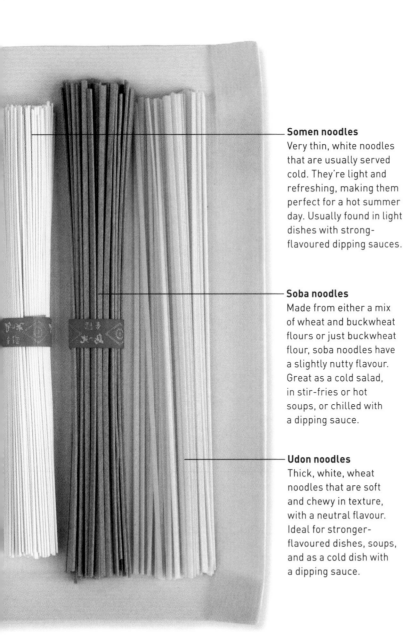

Somen noodles
Very thin, white noodles that are usually served cold. They're light and refreshing, making them perfect for a hot summer day. Usually found in light dishes with strong-flavoured dipping sauces.

Soba noodles
Made from either a mix of wheat and buckwheat flours or just buckwheat flour, soba noodles have a slightly nutty flavour. Great as a cold salad, in stir-fries or hot soups, or chilled with a dipping sauce.

Udon noodles
Thick, white, wheat noodles that are soft and chewy in texture, with a neutral flavour. Ideal for stronger-flavoured dishes, soups, and as a cold dish with a dipping sauce.

WHAT'S IN A NOODLE?

Two ingredients (or three, in the case of the egg noodle) play a vital role in ramen noodles. High-gluten flour provides the structure, kansui water lends to the texture of the noodle, and egg yolks help with the elasticity.

Flour
A wide variety of flours and starches are used in Asia for everything from thickening sauces to making noodles, pastries, buns, and tempura. In Japan, flours high in gluten are referred to as strong-strength flour, while flours low in gluten are referred to as weak-strength flour. For ramen noodles, high-gluten flour is used for a stronger noodle.

Kansui Water
Otherwise known as "lye water", kansui was traditionally found in well water used to make ramen noodles, but is now available in pre-packaged bottles. Kansui gives the noodles their distinctive texture, bounce, flavour, and colour, and is the key element that sets ramen noodles apart.

Kansui water contains sodium, potassium carbonate, and phosphate. It isn't always readily available outside of Japan, so instead, cooks use baked baking soda, which lends the same qualities to the noodles. The recipe for fresh ramen noodles given in this book uses baked bicarbonate of soda instead of kansui water.

Eggs
Some ramen noodle recipes call for eggs, while some don't. Just egg yolks are also sometimes added and lend a nice consistency and elasticity to the dough.

TAKiNG STOCK OF THE STOCK

Stock is the foundation of a bowl of ramen, lovingly transformed in a subsequent step into the broth that will cradle all other ramen ingredients. While stock used to be defined as bone-based, because of vegetarian stocks, it's now considered simply a pre-broth, as it has not yet been seasoned. It's a blank slate, ready to be turned into a broth by adding the appropriate seasonings.

INGREDIENTS

Many of the bone stocks require proteins for the body of the stock. These stocks also need kombu (sea kelp) and aromatics to impart flavour to them.

Proteins in ramen stock include chicken and pork bones. When boiled or simmered for a long time, the collagen in the bones breaks down and gives the stock its viscosity.

Protein in the form of meat in stock imparts flavour to the liquid. For instance, kombu dashi contains bonito flakes (dried, flaked skipjack tuna), which provides the lovely fragrant flavour in kombu dashi stock. There's also a certain amount of fat that's rendered in meat-based stocks. This rendering provides a boost to the flavour, as well as the texture, of the stock.

Dashi stock
Commonly referred to as kombu dashi, this light, fragrant stock is quick and easy to make. Dashi stock is a great base for many ramen dishes.

Chicken stock
This is a flavoursome and comforting base for a variety of ramen dishes. Full of nutrients, it's very versatile and can be used for soups, sauces, and stews.

Kombu is a sea vegetable often used for ramen. Kombu dashi stock, the simplest stock to make, only contains kombu and bonito flakes. Kombu dashi is simmered only for a short time in order to keep the delicate bonito from breaking down too much. Kombu is thought to be high in umami, and produces a lovely tea-like flavour and consistency.

Aromatics used for ramen include carrots, garlic, onion, ginger, shallots, spring onions, leeks, and apples. Variations of these ingredients are typically used for pork, chicken, and vegetarian stocks. The flavours of these ingredients impart different qualities to the ramen; for example, carrots have sweetness to them, while green apples provide sweet and sour notes, and ginger lends a spicy quality. Aromatics need to be simmered or boiled in liquid for enough time to infuse the liquid with flavour. Charring certain aromatics, such as onions, can give ramen a nice, smoky flavour.

STOCK PROFiLES

Ramen stock is classified in a few different ways, one of which is heaviness versus lightness.

Kotteri

A kotteri stock is rich and thick. Tonkotsu is a perfect example of a kotteri stock.

Assari

These stocks are thin, light, and clear. A good example of an assari broth is kombu dashi.

Double stock

This refers to two different stocks being combined, such as chicken and pork. It allows for a more complex flavour and higher level of umami.

Pork stock
This stock gets its milky-white colour from boiling bones for a long period of time. Making pork stock is a labour of love and requires both time and patience.

Vegetarian stock
This is easy to make and is a great alternative to meat-based stocks. Flavoursome, light, and refreshing, vegetable stocks can be made from a wide range of ingredients.

iT'S ALL ABOUT THE BROTH

Ramen broth is arguably the most important element of the dish. The process of converting a basic stock into a unique broth involves adding the appropriate seasoning and flavours for the broth you're trying to achieve. This process imbues the stock with different tastes, textures, and umami factors for each ramen recipe.

CREATING RAMEN BROTH

Tare

This is a seasoning liquid in which ingredients such as miso, soy, salt, and seaweed are mixed, boiled into a concentrated form, and then added to the bottom of a bowl of ramen. The stock is then added and mixed to form the broth. This allows for different flavour preferences based on the tare, not the stock.

Just as acceptable – and much easier for the home cook – is seasoning the broth directly before ladling it into bowls, which is the approach taken in this book. The benefit of not using tare is that you can season the broth precisely, and also fill the bowl with the noodles first.

Shio tare

Shio tare is the oldest and most traditional base for seasoning ramen. Shio translates to *salt,* and can refer to a wide variety of salts, as well as salt derived from the reduction of dashi or seaweed.

Miso

Miso is a complex fermented bean paste, and is considered the most recent ramen seasoning included in the three main categories (the other two being salt and soy sauce). Hearty and pungent, miso is a great base for kotteri broths.

Shoyu

Shoyu is a soy sauce-based seasoning. It can refer to a wide variety of pure soy sauces, or a more concentrated, boiled-down soy sauce. Shoyu tare is mainly used to season assari stocks.

SALT

Salt transforms a stock into a broth and is used in some form as seasoning in every broth, be it Japanese or French. From miso paste to soy sauce, all of the traditional ingredients used to season stocks to make them broths contain some level of salt.

VEGETABLES

There's no end of veggies that can be used in ramen broth. Mushrooms provide earthy flavours and great texture, while sweetcorn provides a lovely, sweet crunch. Bok choy, spinach, and other leafy greens are healthy additions to a dish, and make a beautiful presentation.

PROTEINS

Proteins added to the broth can be one of the main highlights of the dish. From rich bacon to light tofu, proteins alter and enhance the flavour, as well as provide contrasting texture to the dish.

FRUITS

Fruit is used consistently in the recipes throughout this book. Fruit can provide an extra layer of flavour and a touch of acidity that can highlight other flavours – for example, tomato can bring emphasis to the saltiness of miso.

ADDITIONAL AROMATICS

Using additional aromatics such as garlic, ginger, shallots, or carrots can enhance the broth and set the flavour profile of the dish.

BALANCING FLAVOURS

The following are some broth-accompanying ingredients you can add based on the four S's of flavour: sweet, salty, sour, and spicy. However, some ingredients can span a couple of categories. Pineapple juice, for example, brings both sweet and sour profiles.

SWEET

Sugar, brown sugar, sake, mirin, tamarind concentrate, apples, tomatoes, pineapple juice

SPICY

Curry powder, harissa, Thai green curry paste, Thai red curry paste, chillies, chilli black bean paste

SALTY

Miso (all types), dark soy sauce, white soy sauce, fish sauce, kelp

SOUR

Lime juice, vinegar, kimchi, tomatoes, pineapple juice

FATS

The fats can give ramen added flavour, as well as body and a rich sensation. Sesame oil is a great example of a fat that gives a broth tons of flavour while also building a bit of body. Tahini, coconut milk, peanut butter, and soya milk are also good additions to broth that contribute to the overall experience of eating a finished bowl of ramen.

TOPPINGS

Part of the appeal of ramen is the beauty of the presentation. The toppings are all neatly arranged and portray myriad colours, including golden yellow sweetcorn, dark green nori sheets, and white-and-pink narutomaki. Toppings can help create a well-balanced dish by adding texture and building on the all-important four S's of flavour (sweet, salty, sour, and spicy).

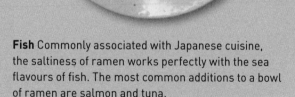

PROTEINS

Proteins are one of the main focal points in a bowl of ramen and provide a richness and meatiness that are in sharp contrast to the base of broth and noodles.

Bacon A wonderful addition to ramen, bacon's high umami content complements and perfectly adds to the flavour of the broth.

Cheese Many different types of cheese work with numerous ramen dishes. For instance, parmesan – which is high in umami – lends a rich, sharp flavour that can go really well with different types of ramen.

Chicken Known for its versatility, chicken can be prepared in myriad ways to give your ramen a flavour boost.

Chinese sausage A broad term for sausages made in China. They can be fresh or dried, lean or fatty. The most popular type is a thin, sweet, dried version. They can often be found in specialty supermarkets.

Duck Rich and full of taste, duck can nicely offset a lighter ramen broth.

Eggs Perhaps one of the most-loved ramen toppings, soft-boiled eggs, marinated or not, are a fabulous addition to a bowl of ramen. The soft egg yolk provides extra body to the broth, the marinated outer egg provides a tangy soy sauce flavour, and the white-and-yellow colours add a punch of colour to the presentation.

Fish Commonly associated with Japanese cuisine, the saltiness of ramen works perfectly with the sea flavours of fish. The most common additions to a bowl of ramen are salmon and tuna.

Narutomaki Also called *naruto*, this white fish cake has a red or pink spiral pattern in the centre. The name stems from the spiral, which resembles the naturally occurring whirlpools in the Naruto Strait. The fish cake is a beautiful addition to a bowl of ramen. You can purchase long sticks of naruto and slice them in small rounds to garnish your ramen.

Chashu pork A common topping for ramen, chashu can be made from either pork belly or pork loin. The staple ingredients in chashu are soy sauce, sugar, sake, and mirin, although you can add other flavours.

Shellfish Many different types of shellfish can be added to ramen, from prawn to scallops.

Tofu Made from soy, tofu has a spongy, cheese-like quality to it.

BALANCiNG TOPPiNGS

As you know, Asian cooking seeks to balance those four S's of flavour. So while you can choose from many different proteins, fruits, or vegetables as toppings for your ramen, make sure you're putting together a balanced dish.

For instance, you don't want to use only ingredients that are salty to flavour your ramen. You also want to avoid using only ingredients with the same, or similar, textures or appearance. When topping a bowl of ramen, plan to incorporate a variety of colours, flavours, and textures. That way, you'll create a ramen that not only tastes great, but is also well balanced.

VEGETABLES AND FRUiTS

Veggies and fruits are an important addition to ramen and can bring fresh flavours, various textures, beautiful colour, and contrasting lightness to the dish.

Bok choy A type of Chinese cabbage, bok choy adds a pop of colour and drama to a bowl of ramen.

Brussels sprouts Part of the emerging fusion ramen trend, which introduces exciting new toppings to the dish, the sharp taste of Brussels sprouts is a real winner when combined with more mellow flavours.

Sweetcorn The contrast between the sweetness of fresh corn and the saltiness of ramen broth is a perfect combination.

Fresh or pickled radishes With their strong, sweet flavour, radishes add a sharp tang to ramen.

Mushrooms Earthy, flavoursome, and healthy, these are a common and excellent addition to ramen. For instance, shiitakes are known to be high on the umami scale and add a meaty texture.

Mustard greens When raw, mustard greens give a dish a spicy component. However, when cooked, they are mild and flavoursome.

Pickled vegetables These add balance to a dish of ramen, offsetting the saltiness with sour.

Red peppers These peppers can lend a sweet, almost fruity taste to your ramen.

Spinach This can add a bit of bitterness and a delicate texture to a bowl of ramen.

Bean sprouts A traditional topping in Asian cuisine, bean sprouts are thin enough that they lightly cook when added in fresh to the broth, while still retaining a slight crunch.

Menma These fermented bamboo shoots have a mellow, woody flavour. They can be simmered in a variety of liquids for extra flavour and give a bowl of ramen a nice contrasting texture.

Apples From sweet to tart, apples lend a mild flavour along with a crunchy texture.

Tamarind Often used in Indian-style sauces or curries, this fruit provides great flavour and a sweet, pungent taste to ramen.

Tomatoes High on the umami scale, tomatoes can bring a rich, sweet, and acidic flavouring to a bowl of ramen.

FiNAL FLOURiSHES

It's almost time to slurp down your ramen, but before you do, you'll need to add some finishing touches. These final additions not only add visual appeal to the dish, but also contribute to and enhance the overall flavour profile.

BODY BUILDERS

Oils and fats can add flavour and richness to a broth, and are often drizzled on top of a steaming bowl of ramen. Oils are a very popular condiment for ramen. Sesame oil, burnt garlic oil, and chilli oil are a few of the most loved oils used to enhance flavour. However, use them in moderation, as many of them have a strong taste.

Burnt garlic oil
Burnt garlic oil, called *mayu* in Japan, balances rich dishes with a slightly bitter flavour.

Butter
A knob of butter is a common addition to ramen in various regions in Japan. Adding body and depth, butter goes well with miso-based ramen, as well as sweetcorn ramen. For a dairy-free alternative, use a nut butter, such as peanut butter or cashew butter.

Chilli oil
Bright reddish-orange chilli oil looks beautiful dotted in a bowl of ramen and provides a bit of heat.

Sesame oil
Sesame oil lends a distinctive earthy flavour to ramen.

Different oils can add richness and body to ramen.

FiNiSHiNG SPRiNKLES

There are many different finishing touches that can propel a good bowl of ramen into something really special. Nuts, flakes, citrus, seeds, and spice can all add oomph to a dish of ramen by providing texture and flavour.

Sesame seeds
Sesame seeds provide a great texture contrast. Toasted sesame seeds bring a unique additional flavour to a bowl of ramen.

Cashews and peanuts
Whole, chopped, or creamed, cashews and peanuts can make wonderful additions to ramen.

Lime wedges
Lime juice adds an acidic and sour profile, which helps bring out other flavours in a bowl of ramen.

Crushed chilli flakes
These bring a level of heat to a bowl of ramen that can help balance the dish and add a level of complexity.

Bonito flakes
Preserved and shaved dried skipjack tuna, these are used to make dashi stock, as well as for flavouring and garnish.

ASSEMBLING A BOWL OF RAMEN

Assembling a bowl of ramen should be done as rapidly as possible to retain heat and to keep the noodles from overcooking due to sitting in the broth too long. In order to quickly put together a bowl of ramen, all of the toppings and garnishes should be prepared, portioned, and the correct temperature.

1 BOWL AND NOODLES

A ramen bowl should be deep and wide, in order to fill it with the noodles and broth and neatly display all of the toppings and garnishes. Clay bowls work the best, as they help retain heat well, followed by ceramic or plastic. There's no need to preheat the bowl, as long as your broth is piping hot.

A portion of uncooked noodles is 110–170g (4–6oz) per person. Cook the noodles minimally, according to the directions, so they retain their chewy, springy texture. Rinse the cooked noodles briefly under room-temperature water to eliminate any gumminess, and then divide them among the bowls.

2 BROTH

Some chefs fill the ramen bowl with a tare (seasoning liquid) and stock first, but other chefs season the entire stock prior to ladling it into the bowl. It's easier to adjust and control the seasoning by adding it to the broth first, so this method is used throughout the book. You should just cover the noodles with the broth; this creates a platform for the toppings. After ladling the hot broth into the bowl, fluff the noodles slightly with a pair of tongs to ensure they aren't sticking together.

3 PROTEIN

It's important to neatly arrange the toppings to create a colourful and appealing display. The toppings should be arranged in differentiated sections, starting with the protein. If the broth just covers the noodles, the toppings should all sit nicely on top, without falling under the broth. If you're adding chashu pork, 2–3 slices are typically enough for a serving.

4 VEGETABLES

After arranging your protein, add the vegetables so they also sit in neat piles on top of the noodles. The vegetables used should complement the broth and the other ingredients. They should provide a contrasting texture, and a nice presentation.

You can use raw or cooked, in-season vegetables for your ramen. Sometimes, vegetables are even cooked in the broth, strained, and then added as a topping.

5 FINAL FLOURISHES

While there's no limit to what final flourishes you add, it's important to have a harmonious balance between what you choose. Spring onions are a common final flourish for ramen. One tablespoon of spring onions is a standard amount, but you can base the amount on personal preference. For a beautiful final touch, finish the bowl by tucking a sheet of nori halfway into the broth against the edge of the bowl.

PLANNiNG AHEAD

Making ramen can be time-consuming due to all of the necessary components of the dish. Some of these are best prepared the day before you plan to serve the ramen, so it's important to read through each recipe before you start in order to make sure you understand what you'll need to do and to allocate the proper time for tackling it.

iTEMS TO HAVE READY BEFORE STARTiNG

The most important item to have ready before starting is the stock. Whether it's a quick stock or an all-day affair, the stock should be finished before you begin the ramen. Making a big batch of stock ahead of time and then freezing it is an ideal way to ensure you always have backup and can quickly make a bowl of ramen. Also important to have ready beforehand are items such as chashu, which takes some time to prepare. Other items that you can make in advance include marinated soft-boiled eggs, menma, and noodles.

COOK AND PREP TiMES FOR COMPONENTS

This chart gives the approximate overall times for making all the basic recipes and stocks in this book. Make any of these components that your dish calls for in advance of making the dish itself.

Tonkotsu Pork Stock: 13 hours

Chashu Pork Belly: 12 hours

Chicken Stock: 6 hours

Marinated Soft-Boiled Eggs: 4 to 12 hours

Ramen Noodles: 3.5 hours

Chashu Pork Loin: 3 hours

Quick Pork Stock: 3 hours

Quick Chicken Stock: 2 hours

Secondary Dashi Stock: 1.5 hours

Vegetarian Stock: 1 to 9 hours

Menma: 40 minutes

Dashi Stock: 30 minutes

Soft-Boiled Eggs: 21 minutes

HOW TO PREPARE

After deciding which recipe to make, take note of the bolded items within the recipe ingredients list, which are the components you'll need to make first. The bolded items all have corresponding recipes within this book, which will show you step-by-step how to prepare them. Make a list of the ingredients you'll need, for both the bolded items and the ramen recipe, and read through to make sure you have all the necessary kitchen equipment.

Once you're ready to begin the dish, make sure everything is chopped, prepared, and ready to go before beginning to cook. This will ensure the cooking and assembling process goes smoothly and quickly. You may need to plan a day ahead for some of the dishes, depending on what stock and toppings you choose.

THE CHEAT GUIDE!

• If you're short on time, the fastest recipes to make are the dashi- and vegetarian-based recipes, as those stocks are simple and quick.

• When it comes to the marinated eggs, one technique for expediting the process is to omit all marinade ingredients except for the soy sauce, and let the eggs sit for only 15–20 minutes. With no water or other ingredients, the marinating process takes much less time.

• Noodles, stocks, and chashu can all be made in large quantities in advance, then frozen until you need them.

CHOOSING YOUR RAMEN

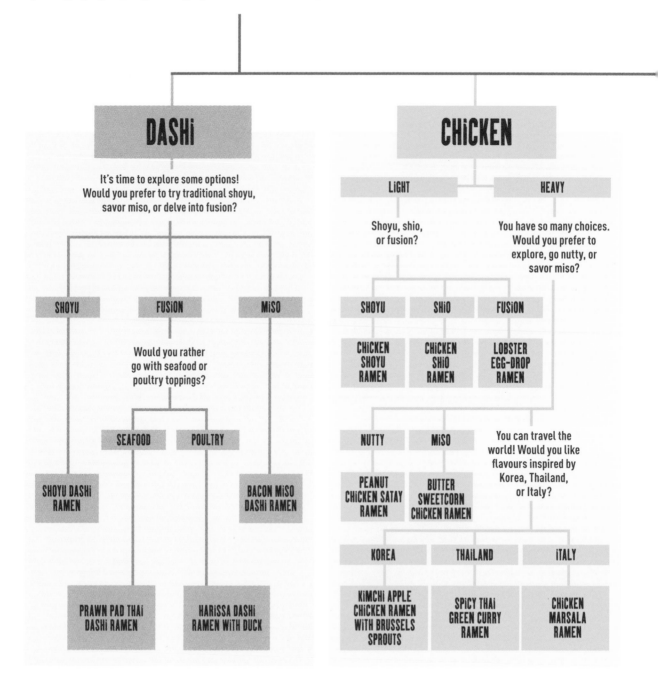

DASHI

It's time to explore some options!
Would you prefer to try traditional shoyu,
savor miso, or delve into fusion?

SHOYU   **FUSION**   **MISO**

Would you rather
go with seafood or
poultry toppings?

SEAFOOD   **POULTRY**

SHOYU DASHI RAMEN

BACON MISO DASHI RAMEN

PRAWN PAD THAI DASHI RAMEN

HARISSA DASHI RAMEN WITH DUCK

CHICKEN

LIGHT   **HEAVY**

Shoyu, shio,
or fusion?

You have so many choices.
Would you prefer to
explore, go nutty, or
savor miso?

SHOYU   **SHIO**   **FUSION**

CHICKEN SHOYU RAMEN

CHICKEN SHIO RAMEN

LOBSTER EGG-DROP RAMEN

NUTTY   **MISO**

You can travel the
world! Would you like
flavours inspired by
Korea, Thailand,
or Italy?

PEANUT CHICKEN SATAY RAMEN

BUTTER SWEETCORN CHICKEN RAMEN

KOREA   **THAILAND**   **ITALY**

KIMCHI APPLE CHICKEN RAMEN WITH BRUSSELS SPROUTS

SPICY THAI GREEN CURRY RAMEN

CHICKEN MARSALA RAMEN

Having trouble deciding where to get started with ramen? Do you have a stock ready but no idea what dish you'd like to create with it? Simply answer the questions in this handy chart, and you'll be well on your way to finding the perfect ramen for you!

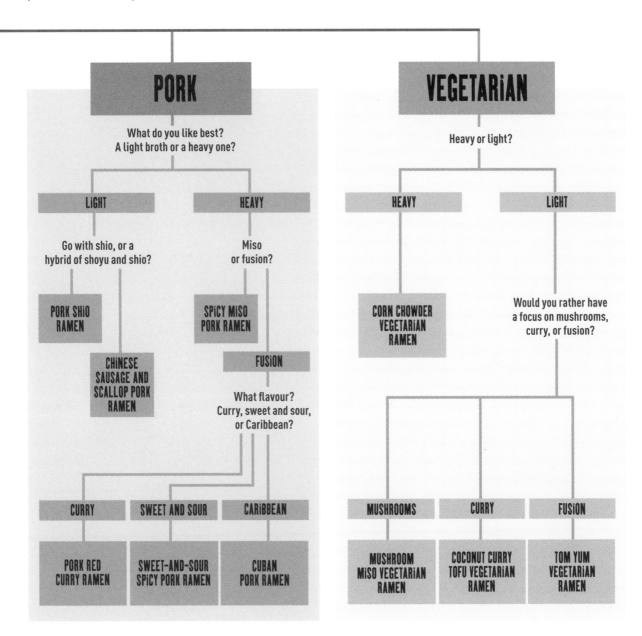

PORK

What do you like best?
A light broth or a heavy one?

LIGHT

Go with shio, or a hybrid of shoyu and shio?

PORK SHIO RAMEN

CHINESE SAUSAGE AND SCALLOP PORK RAMEN

HEAVY

Miso or fusion?

SPICY MISO PORK RAMEN

FUSION

What flavour?
Curry, sweet and sour, or Caribbean?

CURRY

SWEET AND SOUR

CARIBBEAN

PORK RED CURRY RAMEN

SWEET-AND-SOUR SPICY PORK RAMEN

CUBAN PORK RAMEN

VEGETARIAN

Heavy or light?

HEAVY

CORN CHOWDER VEGETARIAN RAMEN

LIGHT

Would you rather have a focus on mushrooms, curry, or fusion?

MUSHROOMS

CURRY

FUSION

MUSHROOM MISO VEGETARIAN RAMEN

COCONUT CURRY TOFU VEGETARIAN RAMEN

TOM YUM VEGETARIAN RAMEN

BASIC RECIPES

This chapter provides the building blocks you need to create your perfect ramen dish, with information on broths; recipes for noodles, chashu, and menma; and ways to prepare eggs and vegetables.

RAMEN NOODLES

Making your own noodles isn't as daunting as you might think. The main difference between regular noodles and ramen noodles is the presence of alkalinized water, which is known as kansui in Japan. You can either make your own kansui with bicarbonate of soda as in this recipe, or buy a ready-made solution. To ensure accuracy when making these noodles, measure the noodle's dry ingredients in grams.

Prep time 2 hours   **Cook time** 1.5 hours
Yield 4 x 170g (6oz) portions

Ingredients:

4tbsp bicarbonate of soda

240ml (8fl oz) warm water

20g (¾oz) sea salt

600g (1lb 5oz) unbleached bread flour

4 egg yolks

Special Equipment:

Stand mixer with dough hook

Rolling pin

Dough roller and portioner

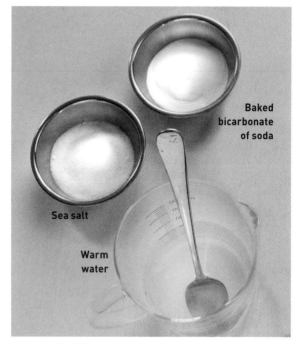

Baked bicarbonate of soda

Sea salt

Warm water

1 To make baked bicarbonate of soda, on a small baking tray lined with greaseproof paper, spread bicarbonate of soda in a thin layer. Bake at 140°C (275°F) for 1.5 hours. Cool, and transfer to a sealed container. Be careful not to touch it when transferring to a container, as it may irritate skin.

2 To make kansui, in a medium measuring cup, combine warm water, sea salt, and 13g baked bicarbonate of soda. Stir to dissolve.

Kansui: if you're using a ready-made kansui solution, substitute the baked bicarbonate of soda in this recipe for 2 tablespoons of the solution.

3 Place the unbleached bread flour in the bowl of an electric mixer. Make a well in the centre of the flour. Put the egg yolks inside the well, then mix with the mixer on low for 2 minutes, until you see the egg yolks distributed throughout the flour.

4 Add the kansui and mix until the flour starts to pull away from the sides of the bowl. Once fully incorporated, start kneading the dough by hand in the bowl. (The mixture is relatively dry and can be difficult for a mixer engine.) Add more water if needed. Add 1 tablespoon of water at a time – just enough to help the dough stick together. The dough should come together without being moist to the touch.

Continued ➜

5 Once the dough is holding together, take it out of the bowl and knead it by hand on a flat surface until smooth, about 5–10 minutes. Wrap the dough in cling film and leave it to rest for at least 1 hour.

Storage: Wrap each noodle bundle in cling film, place in a sealable plastic bag, and refrigerate. The dough will last up to 1 week in the refrigerator and up to 1 month in the freezer.

6 Take the dough out of the cling film and roll it out using a rolling pin, until it is thin enough to be run through a dough roller.

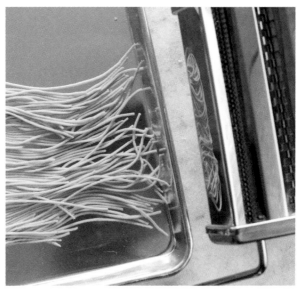

8 Run the dough through a pasta cutter, at roughly 2mm (¼in) thickness.

7 Starting off slowly, run the dough through the dough roller on each setting 3 times each, up until, and including, setting 4. At this point, especially if your dough is moist, leave it exposed on a table to dry out slightly before cutting it.

9 This gives you beautiful, straight noodles. (Curly noodles require special equipment.) Cut the dough into roughly 35cm (14in) lengths of noodles.

COOKING FRESH RAMEN NOODLES

The texture of the noodles in ramen dishes is very important. You can have a delicious broth, but if your noodles are soggy, it will ruin the meal. Cooked ramen noodles should be firm and chewy. Make sure your pot is large enough so the noodles are not overcrowded.

Prep time 5 mins   **Cook time** 2 mins
Yield 4 bowls

Ingredients:
4.75l (8 pints) tap water
680g (24oz) fresh **Ramen Noodles**

Special Equipment:
Deep pot, 7.5l (13 pints) or larger
Colander
4 deep serving bowls

1 In a 7.5l (13 pint) or larger pan over a medium-high heat, boil the tap water. You should have at least 240ml (8fl oz) of water for every 25g (1oz) of noodles. Don't salt the water; the noodles themselves already contain salt, as will the ramen broth.

2 When the water comes to the boil, sprinkle the Ramen Noodles into the pan, spreading them around with tongs to ensure they don't stick.

Cold-Dish Noodles: if you intend to use the noodles for a cold dish such as a tsukemen (dipping ramen) or noodle salad, rinse them under cold water immediately after straining to stop them from cooking any further.

3 Cook the noodles for 50 seconds, stirring occasionally with the tongs to prevent the noodles from sticking to each other.

4 Turn off the burner and drain the noodles into a colander. Rinse them quickly under lukewarm water for 10 seconds, and then shake the colander to drain.

5 Using the tongs, divide the noodles between 4 deep serving bowls.

CHASHU PORK LOIN

Packed with umami, thin strips of chashu pork loin are often saved for last when eating ramen, as if saving the best fireworks for the finale. Making chashu pork loin is simple and hugely rewarding. The delicious broth can be saved and used for marinated eggs, seasoning (tare), reheating chashu slices, and garnishing.

Prep time 25 mins   **Cook time** 2.5 hours
Yield 1kg (2lb) pork loin

Storage: You can wrap any leftover unsliced chashu pork loin in cling film and store it in the fridge for up to 1 week. Slice only as many pieces as you need at one time and keep the rest in the fridge until you are ready to use it.

Ingredients:

1kg (2lb) pork loin

2 tsp sea salt

2 tbsp vegetable oil

240ml (8fl oz) water

240ml (8fl oz) soy sauce

240ml (8fl oz) sake

240ml (8fl oz) mirin

85g (3oz) dark brown sugar, tightly packed

5 cloves garlic, crushed

5 spring onions, roughly chopped

5cm (2in) knob ginger, peeled and sliced

2 tbsp lime juice

Special Equipment:

Butcher's twine

1 Lay the pork loin on a chopping board. Roll and tie it into a log shape using butcher's twine, then rub it with the sea salt.

2 Heat the vegetable oil in a large frying pan over a high heat. Add the pork loin and sear on all sides, turning it with tongs, for about 10 minutes.

3 Add the water, soy sauce, sake, mirin, dark brown sugar, garlic, spring onions, ginger, and lime juice. Bring to the boil.

4 Reduce the heat to low. Cover the pan with foil, pressing down to cover most of the pork loin and liquid, but allowing some steam to escape. Simmer for 2 hours.

5 Remove the pork loin, place on a chopping board, and rest for 15 minutes. On a medium heat, bring the braising liquid up to a simmer, and reduce for approximately 5–8 minutes, until it thickens slightly and can lightly coat the back of a spoon. Remove from the heat. Allow to cool before using it as a seasoning or marinade.

6 After the meat has cooled, roll it tightly in cling film to help it retain its shape and keep the moisture in. Store it in the fridge. When you're ready to use it, unwrap and slice it very thinly in rounds. That way, when you add it to the broth, the liquid will heat it through.

CHASHU PORK BELLY

Succulent slices of chashu pork belly are a welcome and delicious addition to most ramen dishes. Rich and hearty, with a high fat content, the pork belly is best seared before being added to the dish. One unique addition here is coconut milk, which marries well with the pork.

Prep time 8.5 hours   **Cook time** 3.5 hours
Yield 1kg (2lb) pork belly

Storage: Chashu pork belly will keep in the fridge for up to 1 week if placed in a sealed plastic bag. it will also freeze well (for up to 6 months) if properly wrapped in a sealed plastic freezer bag.

Ingredients:

1kg (2lb) slab pork belly, skin off

1 tbsp sea salt

1 tbsp sesame oil

480ml (16fl oz) **Chicken Stock**

4 tbsp white soy sauce

2 tbsp sake

2 tbsp mirin

1 tbsp sugar

5 cloves garlic, crushed

5 spring onions, roughly chopped

5cm (2in) knob ginger, peeled and sliced

2 tbsp lime juice

390ml can coconut milk

Special Equipment:

Large ovenproof dish

1 Heat the oven to 150°C (300°F). Lay the pork belly on a chopping board, and rub with the salt. If you have a large piece, you can roll and tie the belly into a log with butcher's twine.

2 In a large ovenproof dish, combine the sesame oil, Chicken Stock, white soy sauce, sake, mirin, sugar, garlic, spring onions, ginger, lime juice, and coconut milk. Transfer the pork belly to the dish, fat side up.

3 Cover the dish tightly with foil, and cook for 3.5 hours. Test for doneness by inserting a knife – the meat should be tender enough to fall apart easily. Take the pork belly out of the oven, and leave to cool and rest for 1 hour to absorb the juices.

4 Carefully transfer the pork belly to a greaseproof paper-lined baking sheet. Place another piece of greaseproof paper on top, then another baking sheet on that. Finally, place something heavy on top to weight it. Transfer to the fridge. Strain the juices and reserve for another use, such as seasoning your ramen.

5 Leave to sit overnight in the fridge. This will ensure the pork belly is uniform and easy to slice. When you are ready to use it, place the pork belly on a chopping board and slice it into 2.5cm (1in) thick pieces that are roughly 7.5–10cm (3–4in) long.

6 Before adding to your ramen, you will need to sear it to crisp it up and heat it through. Heat a non-stick or cast-iron pan on a medium-high heat, and add a bit of vegetable oil. Sprinkle the pork belly slices with a dash of salt, and add them to the pan. Sear until golden brown.

SOFT-BOiLED EGGS

Soft-boiled eggs, also known as 6-minute eggs, are a fantastic addition to ramen dishes. These eggs can either be used as is, or marinated for extra flavour.

Prep time 15 mins **Cook time** 6 mins **Yield** 4 eggs

Ingredients:

1.4l (2½ pints) water

4 eggs

Special Equipment:

Ice bath

Timer

Storage: Eggs will keep in the fridge for up to 1 week. Before using the cooked eggs for ramen, let them come to room temperature, then slice in half lengthways.

1 Fill a medium pan two-thirds full of water. Place over a high heat and bring to the boil.

2 Prepare an ice bath for the eggs. Fill a medium bowl with cold water and ½ cup ice.

3 Gently lower the eggs into the boiling water with a slotted spoon. Cook for exactly 6 minutes.

4 Turn off the heat. Immediately transfer the eggs with the slotted spoon to the ice bath. Leave to stand for at least 10 minutes.

5 Remove the eggs from the ice bath, and carefully peel them. You may use them as is, or move on to the steps to make Marinated Soft-Boiled Eggs.

MARiNATED SOFT-BOiLED EGGS

These delicious eggs are a staple in ramen. The soft yolk adds body to the broth, and the marinated whites provide a great additional texture. You can add them to virtually any ramen dish!

Prep time 4–12 hours   **Yield** 4 eggs

Ingredients:

120ml (4fl oz) soy sauce

2 tbsp sake

1 tbsp sugar

1 tbsp mirin

240ml (8fl oz) water

4 **Soft-Boiled Eggs**, peeled

Special Equipment:

Medium sealable plastic bag

Storage: Once eggs have been marinated, they will keep in the fridge for up to 1 week.

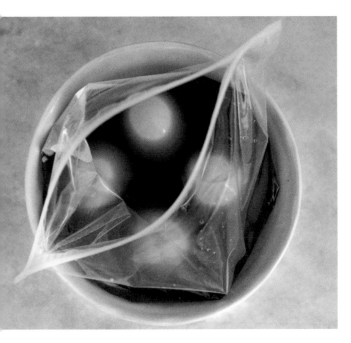

Prepare the marinade by placing a medium sealable plastic bag into a medium bowl and filling it with the soy sauce, sake, sugar, mirin, and water. Stir to dissolve the sugar. Add the Soft-Boiled Eggs to the marinade. Press the air out of the bag and seal. Refrigerate for at least 4 hours, but no more than 12 hours. Before using the eggs for ramen, let them come to room temperature, then slice in half lengthways.

CUTTING SOFT-BOILED EGGS

Cutting a soft boiled egg in half without making a mess of the yolk can sometimes prove to be a challenge. A cheese cutter will provide the cleanest and easiest cut, but if you do not have one available you can use fishing line, unflavoured dental floss, or a sharp knife.

Special Equipment:

A cheese cutter, fishing line, unflavoured dental floss, or a sharp knife

If you're using fishing line or dental floss, tie one end of the line to something and hold the other end very taut with one hand. Cup the egg lightly in your other hand; bring it up to the line, floss, or harp; and slice through.

If you're using a knife, place the egg on a chopping board. Start slowly with a slicing motion and then finish quickly.

MENMA

Menma is a condiment made from bamboo shoots. It's used in many different types of ramen and is considered a favourite topping in Japan. Although ready-made menma is available in Asian grocery stores, making your own is simple and rewarding.

Prep time 20 mins   **Cook time** 20 mins   **Yield** 350g (12oz)

Ingredients:

1 garlic clove, finely chopped

1 tbsp sake

2 tbsp soy sauce

4tbsp water

1 tsp sugar

1 tsp rice wine vinegar

2 tsp sesame oil

140g can sliced
   bamboo shoots

Garlic

Sugar

Sake

Sesame oil

Soy sauce

Bamboo
shoots

Rice wine
vinegar

1 In a small bowl, combine the sake, soy sauce, water, sugar, and rice wine vinegar. Set aside.

Storage: You don't have to use menma straightaway. You can store it in the fridge for up to 1 week. Simply let the menma cool, then place it in a plastic sealable bag before putting it in the fridge.

2 Heat the oil in a frying pan over a medium heat. Add the bamboo shoots, and fry for 1 minute. Reduce the heat, and add the garlic. Add the ingredients from the bowl.

3 Simmer for 15 minutes, stirring occasionally, until the liquid has mostly evaporated. Transfer to a plate and allow to cool.

BURNT GARLIC OIL

Burnt garlic oil is a fantastic addition to a bowl of ramen. On its own, it can be a bit bitter, but lightly drizzled as a finishing touch, it provides a deep, nutty flavour that creates a lovely contrast to a rich broth.

Prep time 10 mins   **Cook time** 20 mins   **Yield** 120ml (4fl oz)

Storage: For use at a later date, transfer burnt garlic oil to a sealable container and refrigerate for up to 2 months.

Ingredients:

4 tbsp vegetable oil

10 cloves garlic, finely chopped

4 tbsp sesame oil

½ tsp sugar

½ tsp sea salt

Special Equipment:

Food processor or blender

1 In a small saucepan over a medium-low heat, cook the vegetable oil and garlic until it starts to brown.

2 Stirring constantly, reduce the heat to low and cook for 10 minutes.

3 The garlic should look dark and sticky. Once it does, turn off the heat.

4 Add the sesame oil, sugar, and sea salt, and stir to combine.

5 Transfer the mixture to a food processor or blender, and blend until fully incorporated, about 1–2 minutes. The oil is ready to use immediately.

PREPPING VEGETABLES

There's a saying that the sharper your knife, the less you cry. This means if your knife is dull, you risk cutting yourself when the blade slips on the skin of the object instead of slicing straight through. So it's important to have a very sharp chef's knife you're comfortable using. When using a chopping board, place a damp kitchen towel underneath to prevent it from moving.

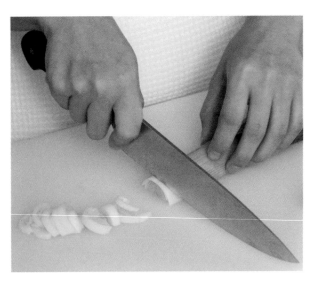

HOLDING THE KNIFE

In order to have complete control over the knife, move your dominant hand up the handle, so your thumb is on one side of the blade and your index finger is on the other side of the blade.

SLICING

Gripping the knife properly, cut straight down on the vegetable, keeping your fingertips tucked out of the way of the blade.

HOLDING THE VEGETABLE

With your non-dominant hand, hold the vegetable you intend to cut in a claw-like grip, enabling the flat part of the knife to rest against your knuckles. This ensures your fingertips stay out of the way of the blade and avoid getting nicked.

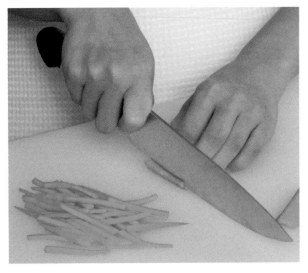

JULIENNING

Once you've cut slices, stack a few of them on top of each other and cut down at regular, short intervals to create thin strips.

DICING

Gather the julienned strips and line them up perpendicular to the knife blade. Cut them into even segments to make cubes.

FINELY CHOPPING

After dicing, pass the knife repeatedly over whatever you're cutting, scraping up and flipping over the pieces to ensure evenness.

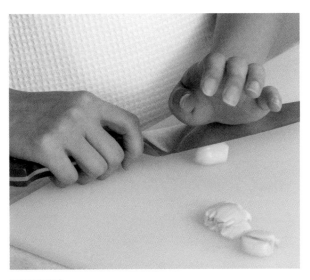

CRUSHING

To crush, lay the flat of the knife on the item, blade pointing away from you. With the heel of your other hand, whack the flat of the knife.

ROUGHLY CHOPPING

Hold the knife in your dominant hand and place the fingers of your other hand on the tip of the knife blade. Gently rock the knife back and forth.

RECiPES WiTH DASHi STOCK

Easy to make, dashi stock has a delicate, tea-like quality that's incredibly versatile. Dashi's fresh sea flavours and subtle undertones pair well with ingredients such as fish, miso, and tofu.

DASHI STOCK

Dashi stock is present in much of Japanese cooking. A good dashi stock is actually incredibly easy to make. This particular one is a kombu dashi, made from kombu (edible kelp) and bonito flakes. The flavour can be described as complex yet subtle and nuanced, almost like a fragrant tea.

Prep time 5 mins **Cook time** 25 mins **Yield** 2l (3½ pints)

Ingredients:

5 x 15.25cm (6in) strips dried kombu (kelp)

2l (3½ pints) water

175g (6oz) packed bonito flakes

Special Equipment:

Fine-mesh strainer or cheesecloth

2 In a large pan over a medium heat, simmer the kombu in water for 15–20 minutes, making sure the water doesn't boil.

1 Gently wipe the kombu strips with a clean kitchen towel or a slightly moist piece of kitchen paper to remove some of the residue, but not all of it, as it lends to the flavour.

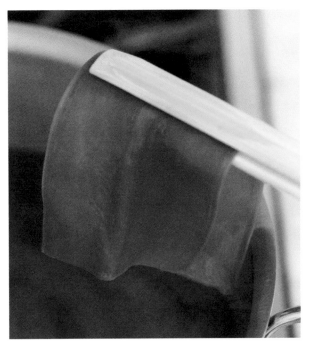

3 Leaving the burner on, remove the kombu from the water with tongs, and place into a large container. (Set aside for Secondary Dashi Stock, if you'd like.)

4 Add the bonito flakes to the kombu water, and gently simmer for 2 minutes.

5 Turn off the heat, and allow the stock to steep for 5 minutes.

Continued →

6 Using a fine-mesh strainer or cheesecloth, strain the liquid into a bowl. The stock should be pale in colour and smell sweet and briny. (Keep the strained bonito flakes for Secondary Dashi Stock, if you'd like.) The stock is now ready to be used immediately.

Storage: Cool the stock, transfer it to a sealable container, and refrigerate it for up to 4 days. You can also freeze this stock for up to 6 months.

Dashi Stock

SECONDARY DASHI STOCK

The previous recipe for dashi stock is honey coloured, clear, and delicate, which is perfect for using in simple ramen dishes that don't have many additions, as the broth will stand on its own. This dashi stock will be slightly cloudy and can have a milder taste, making it good for miso-based soups, sauces, or simmered dishes.

Prep time 1 hour   **Cook time** 20 mins   **Yield** 1l (1¾ pints)

1 In a large pan over a high heat, bring the water, strained kombu strips, and bonito flakes to the boil.

2 Lower the heat to a simmer. Allow to simmer for 10 minutes.

3 Turn off the heat and stir in additional bonito flakes. Allow to steep for 1 hour.

4 Strain through a fine-mesh strainer or cheesecloth. The stock is now ready to be used immediately.

Ingredients:

1l (1¾ pints) water

Strained kombu strips and bonito flakes from **Dashi Stock**

60g (2oz) packed bonito flakes

Special Equipment:

Fine-mesh strainer or cheesecloth

Storage: You can store this stock in the same way as the regular Dashi stock. if freezing, portion it in an ice-cube tray or into 240ml (8fl oz) servings first so you can easily use it.

Secondary **Dashi** Stock

SHOYU DASHI RAMEN

Dashi and shoyu (soy sauce) are a classic ramen combination, delicate and refreshing. This ramen is light but packed with a savoury tang, which will have you polishing off every last drop.

Prep time 20 mins   **Cook time** 20 mins   **Yield** 4 bowls

1.4l (2½ pints) **Dashi Stock**

3 tbsp soy sauce

4 tbsp dry sake

1 tbsp mirin

680g (24oz) fresh **Ramen Noodles**

8 slices **Chashu Pork Loin**, at room temperature

4 **Marinated Soft-Boiled Eggs**, sliced in half lengthways

85g (3oz) **Menma**

2 spring onions, finely chopped

4 sheets nori

1 tbsp shichimi togarashi powder

1 In a large pan over a medium heat, bring the Dashi Stock to a simmer.

2 Add the soy sauce, dry sake, and mirin. Simmer for 5 minutes.

3 In a large pan of boiling water over a high heat, cook the Ramen Noodles for 50 seconds, stirring occasionally. Drain, rinse, and divide between 4 deep serving bowls.

4 Fill the bowls with the hot broth, just covering the noodles.

5 Neatly arrange the Chashu Pork Loin, Marinated Soft-Boiled Eggs, Menma, and spring onions on top of the noodles in each bowl.

6 Tuck 1 nori sheet into the broth against the side of each bowl. Sprinkle the shichimi togarashi powder on the eggs.

TSUKEMEN DASHi RAMEN WiTH CHASHU

Tsukemen – dipping ramen – is a popular variation of ramen, one that's especially enjoyed during hot summer months. Dip the cold or room-temperature noodles into the broth to soak up loads of flavour while staying refreshingly cool.

Prep time 10 mins   **Cook time** 10 mins
Yield 4 bowls

680g (24oz) fresh **Ramen Noodles**
720ml (1¼ pints) **Dashi Stock**
240ml (8fl oz) mirin
240ml (8fl oz) soy sauce
2 tbsp sugar
4 spring onions, finely chopped
2 tbsp vegetable oil
1 tsp sea salt
12 slices **Chashu Pork Belly**
175g (6oz) sliced shiitake mushrooms
4 **Marinated Soft-Boiled Eggs**, sliced in half lengthways
85g (3oz) **Menma**

Special Equipment:
8 serving dishes

1 In a large pan of boiling water over a high heat, cook the Ramen Noodles for 50 seconds, stirring occasionally. Drain, rinse, and divide between 4 serving dishes.

2 In a medium pan over a medium heat, bring the Dashi Stock to a simmer. Add the mirin, soy sauce, sugar, and spring onions. Reduce heat to low, and simmer for 5 minutes.

3 Heat 1 tablespoon vegetable oil in a large frying pan over a medium-high heat. Sprinkle the salt over the Chashu Pork Belly.

4 Sear the Chashu Pork Belly in the pan on both sides, about 2 minutes on each side. (Sear in batches, if necessary.) Remove from the pan and set aside.

5 In the same pan, add the remaining vegetable oil. Add the shiitake mushrooms and sauté until golden, about 5 minutes.

6 Fill 4 bowls with the warm broth. Divide the cooked Chashu Pork Belly and mushrooms, Marinated Soft-Boiled Eggs, and Menma between 4 serving dishes.

7 Serve each guest a bowl of broth, a serving dish of noodles, and a serving dish of garnishes.

Serving Suggestion: You can serve the broth either cold or hot, and include garnishes in the broth, with the noodles, or separately. Dip the noodles into the broth with chopsticks and slurp away!

TEMPURA PRAWN DASHI RAMEN

The Japanese have been cooking tempura since the eighteenth century, after Portuguese missionaries introduced the technique. This dish is filled with a variety of great textures, including crunchy tempura prawns, chewy noodles, and silky broth.

Prep time 35 mins   **Cook time** 25 mins   **Yield** 4 bowls

1l (1¾ pints) vegetable oil

1.4l (2½ pints) **Dashi Stock**

160ml (6fl oz) soy sauce

120ml (4fl oz) mirin

2 tbsp rice wine vinegar

2 tbsp sugar

125g (4½oz) plain flour

180ml (6½fl oz) ice water

1 egg

12 king prawns, peeled and deveined

30g (1oz) cornflour

24oz (680g) fresh **Ramen Noodles**

2 spring onions, thinly sliced

4 slices narutomaki (fish cakes)

85g (3oz) cooked sweetcorn kernels

4 sheets nori

1 tsp shichimi togarashi powder

Special Equipment:

Cooking thermometer

1 In a small deep pan, heat the vegetable oil to 180°C (350°F) according to a thermometer.

2 In a large pan over a medium heat, bring the Dashi Stock to a simmer. Add the soy sauce, mirin, rice wine vinegar, and sugar, and simmer for 5 minutes. Turn off the heat and set aside.

3 In a medium mixing bowl, sift the flour. Remove the ice from the ice water, put the ice water into a small bowl, and vigorously whisk the egg into it.

4 Pour the egg mixture into the bowl of flour, and mix to just combine, being careful not to overmix.

5 Pat dry and lay flat the prawns. Sift the cornflour over both sides. Holding each prawn by the tail, dip into the egg-flour batter, then place in the oil.

6 Fry the prawns until golden brown, about 3 minutes. Remove the prawns with tongs and place on a wire rack or a paper plate lined with kitchen paper.

7 In a large pan of boiling water over a high heat, cook the Ramen Noodles for 50 seconds. Drain, rinse, and divide between 4 deep serving bowls.

8 Reheat the broth to a simmer. Fill the bowls with the hot broth, just covering the noodles. Arrange the prawns, spring onions, narutomaki, and sweetcorn on top of noodles in each bowl.

9 Tuck 1 nori sheet into the side of each bowl. Sprinkle the shichimi togarashi powder over the top.

SPICY MISO DASHI RAMEN WITH SALMON

Fresh salmon is not only extremely tasty, but also a beautiful addition to a bowl of ramen. The dashi stock provides a great base for the salmon, while the fermented red miso paste perfectly complements the sea flavours of this ramen.

Prep time 20 mins   **Cook time** 30 mins
Yield 4 bowls

1.4l (2 ½ pints) **Dashi Stock**

1 tsp sugar

4 tbsp plus 2 tbsp soy sauce

2 tsp sesame oil

2 tbsp rice wine vinegar

4 tbsp red miso paste

2 tbsp spicy fermented chilli bean paste

2 x 170g (6oz) salmon fillets

2 tbsp vegetable oil

680g (24oz) fresh **Ramen Noodles**

85g (3oz) enoki mushrooms, trimmed

2 tbsp white sesame seeds

4 **Marinated Soft-Boiled Eggs**, sliced in half lengthways

2 spring onions, finely chopped

2 tsp chilli oil

1 In a large pan over a medium heat, bring the Dashi Stock to a simmer.

2 Add the sugar, 4 tablespoons soy sauce, sesame oil, rice wine vinegar, red miso paste, and chilli bean paste. Simmer over a low heat for 10 minutes.

3 While the broth is simmering, pat dry the salmon fillets and season with the remaining 2 tablespoons soy sauce.

4 Heat the vegetable oil in a large frying pan over a medium-high heat. Add the salmon fillets.

5 Cook the salmon for 3–5 minutes on each side, until cooked through. Remove the salmon fillets from the pan and set aside.

6 In a large pan of boiling water over a high heat, cook the Ramen Noodles for 50 seconds, stirring occasionally. Drain, rinse, and divide between 4 deep serving bowls.

7 Fill the bowls with the hot broth, just covering the noodles. Break up the salmon fillets into large chunks and divide between the bowls.

8 Neatly arrange the enoki mushrooms, white sesame seeds, Marinated Soft-Boiled Eggs, and spring onions on top of the noodles in each bowl. Sprinkle the chilli oil over the broth.

CHOOSING FISH

Choosing fish can be a daunting process. Fresh or frozen? Supermarket or fish monger? Because the fish you buy is just as important as how you cook it, follow these tips for selecting the right kind for your dish. Once you've purchased your fish, be sure to handle and store it correctly to avoid spoilage.

FRESH FISH

If you are buying fresh fish, make sure it doesn't have any unpleasant odours. It should have a fresh sea smell. Beyond smell, there are some other considerations when making your purchase.

Once you've picked out your fish, cook or freeze it within 2 days of purchase. Fish should be stored in the refrigerator between 0–5°C (32–41°F) and in the freezer at -18°C (0°F) or below for 1–3 months, depending on the type of fish.

When storing the fish, keep it tightly wrapped and in a sealed plastic bag in the fridge.

Fins
The fins should be full, moist, and healthy looking. The fish shouldn't have torn or jagged fins.

Texture
The fish should be firm to the touch, moist, and a little slippery. When you press your finger into the fish, the flesh should spring back immediately and not stay sunken.

Scales
If it's a scaly fish, the scales should lie flat and not be ruffled. The scales should be firmly attached to the skin and none should be missing.

Frozen Fish: Make sure they are thoroughly frozen. Avoid fish that have any signs of freezer burn or ice crystals, which occur when fish have been frozen, thawed, and refrozen. Defrost the fish in the fridge.

TSUKiJi MARKET

In operation since 1935, Tsukiji Market, located in central Tokyo, is Japan's largest and most famous seafood market. Each year, thousands of tourists flock to the market to witness the 2,000 tonnes of fish and seafood being bought and sold every day! The famous tuna auctions take place inside the market, while there's an outer market that houses stalls and restaurants. Over 400 different types of seafood product are sold at the market, as well as fruit, vegetables, meat, flowers, knives, and kitchen equipment.

The market is open from 5am until 2pm. The wholesale auctions are reserved solely for licensed buyers and run until 7am, when the purchased fish is then moved for distribution nationally, or moved to the shops within the market for retail sale. Whole fish are then broken down with extremely large knives or band saws, in an awe-inspiring display.

Eyes
The eyes should be shiny, clear, and bright. If the eyes are cloudy, the fish has begun to deteriorate. The eyes should not be sunken in.

Gills
Check the gills to ensure they are bright red and clean. Gills that are dark and slimy indicate the fish is no longer fresh.

The outer market caters to the public, with fish available to buy in small, non-wholesale-sized quantities.

MUSHROOM TOFU DASHI RAMEN

This healthy dish has a lovely earthy flavour, which is balanced with a bit of heat from the dried chillies. The dish can easily be made vegetarian by using vegetarian stock instead of dashi stock.

Prep time 20 mins **Cook time** 40 mins **Yield** 4 bowls

1.4l (2½ pints) **Dashi Stock**

85g (3oz) dried wood ear mushrooms

175g (6oz) dried shiitake mushrooms

4 garlic cloves, crushed

8 spring onions, finely chopped (reserve some green ends for garnish)

1½ tsp crushed chilli flakes

175g (6oz) firm tofu, cubed

680g (24oz) fresh **Ramen Noodles**

175g (6oz) fresh enoki mushrooms, trimmed

4 slices narutomaki (fish cake)

4 sheets nori, sliced into small strips

Special Equipment:

Fine-mesh strainer

Tongs or chopsticks

1 In a large pan over a medium heat, bring the Dashi Stock to a simmer.

2 Add the dried wood ear mushrooms, dried shiitake mushrooms, garlic, and spring onions, and simmer for 30 minutes.

3 Strain the broth through a fine-mesh strainer, and with tongs or chopsticks, carefully remove the dried mushrooms. Discard the remaining solids, and pour the broth back into the pot.

4 Slice the shiitake mushrooms in half, and the wood ear mushrooms into strips. Return to the broth, and bring to a simmer.

5 Add the crushed chilli flakes and tofu. Simmer for 5 minutes.

6 In a large pan of boiling water over a high heat, cook the Ramen Noodles for 50 seconds, stirring occasionally. Drain, rinse, and divide between 4 deep serving bowls.

7 Fill the bowls with the hot broth, just covering the noodles. Add the enoki mushrooms and narutomaki to each bowl, and sprinkle the nori strips over the top.

Straining Mushroom Grit: Dried mushrooms can be a bit gritty when rehydrated in the broth. Straining the broth after rehydrating the mushrooms can eliminate the grit from the broth while retaining the flavour.

PRAWN PAD THAI DASHI RAMEN

A popular dish in Thailand, pad thai has also become a Western classic. The flavour profile of pad thai is citrusy, bold, and deep, which pairs perfectly with garlicky prawns.

Prep time 20 mins   **Cook time** 20 mins   **Yield** 4 bowls

1.4l (2½ pints) **Dashi Stock**

80ml (2½fl oz) tamarind concentrate

2 tbsp light brown sugar

240ml (8fl oz) soy sauce

3 tbsp lime juice

1 tbsp mirin

2 tsp chilli garlic sauce

4 spring onions, finely chopped

3 tbsp vegetable oil

1 tbsp garlic, finely chopped

285g (10oz) medium-large prawns, peeled and deveined

680g (24oz) fresh **Ramen Noodles**

175g (6oz) bean sprouts, blanched

85g (3oz) chopped peanuts or cashews

2 tbsp chopped coriander

4 lime wedges

1 In a large pan over a medium heat, bring the Dashi Stock to a simmer.

2 Add the tamarind, light brown sugar, soy sauce, lime juice, mirin, chilli garlic sauce, and ½ the spring onions. Simmer for 10 minutes.

3 While the broth is simmering, heat the vegetable oil in a large frying pan over a medium heat.

4 Add the garlic and prawns, and sauté for 4–5 minutes, until cooked through.

5 Remove the prawns from the pan with tongs and place on a plate.

6 In a large pan of boiling water over a high heat, cook the Ramen Noodles for 50 seconds, stirring occasionally. Drain, rinse, and divide between 4 deep serving bowls.

7 Fill the bowls with the hot broth, just covering the noodles.

8 Garnish each bowl with the prawns, remaining spring onions, bean sprouts, chopped peanuts, and coriander. Serve with lime wedges.

HARISSA DASHI RAMEN WITH DUCK

This North African-inspired dish contains harissa, a savoury blend of red peppers, spices, herbs, and lemon and a perfect addition to a hot bowl of ramen. The duck is rich and full of flavour, providing a nice contrast to the light dashi stock.

Prep time 20 mins   **Cook time** 35 mins   **Yield** 4 bowls

1.4l (2½ pints) **Dashi Stock**

6 tbsp soy sauce

6 tbsp prepared harissa

1 tbsp sugar

1 tbsp rice wine vinegar

5 spring onions, thinly sliced (reserve some for garnish)

175g (6oz) shiitake mushrooms, sliced

2x 175g (6oz) duck breasts, skin on

1 tsp sea salt

½ tsp freshly ground black pepper

680g (24oz) fresh **Ramen Noodles**

4 **Marinated Soft-Boiled Eggs**, sliced in half lengthways

2 tbsp white sesame seeds

Scoring Duck Skin: When scoring duck skin, it's important to cut through the skin but not the meat. Scoring the skin will help to render the fat and crisp the skin nicely.

1 In a large pan over a medium heat, bring the Dashi Stock to a simmer. Add the soy sauce, harissa, sugar, rice wine vinegar, spring onions, and shiitake mushrooms. Simmer for 15 minutes.

2 Pat dry the duck breasts with kitchen paper. Score the duck skin in a crisscross pattern. Season with salt and pepper.

3 In a medium pan over a medium-high heat, add the duck breasts, skin-side down, and render the fat for 7–8 minutes. Once the duck skin is brown and crispy, turn the breasts over and cook for 3 minutes.

4 Remove the duck breasts from the pan and let them rest on a plate, skin-side up, for 10 minutes. Reserve the rendered duck fat for a garnish.

5 In a large pan of boiling water over a high heat, cook the Ramen Noodles for 50 seconds, stirring occasionally. Drain, rinse, and divide between 4 deep serving bowls.

6 Fill the bowls with the hot broth, just covering the noodles. Slice the duck breasts on the bias, 2cm (¾in) thick. Divide the duck into 4 portions and fan out the slices on top of the noodles.

7 Neatly arrange the reserved spring onions and Marinated Soft-Boiled Eggs in each bowl. Sprinkle white sesame seeds over the duck. Drizzle 1½ teaspoons rendered duck fat over the toppings of each bowl.

SOYA MiLK DASHi RAMEN

This ramen is light, fragrant, and extremely satisfying. It may just become one of your favourite broths. The soya milk adds a subtle creaminess and blends perfectly with the miso and ginger.

Prep time 15 mins   **Cook time** 15 mins   **Yield** 4 bowls

1.4l (2½ pints) **Dashi Stock**

1 tbsp ginger, finely chopped

3 tbsp white miso paste

1 tsp sugar

3 tbsp white soy sauce

180ml (6½fl oz) soya milk

1 tsp sea salt

680g (24oz) fresh **Ramen Noodles**

4 **Marinated Soft-Boiled Eggs**, sliced in half lengthways

85g (3oz) spring onions, finely chopped

85g (3oz) **Menma**

85g (3oz) cooked sweetcorn kernels

4 small knobs butter (about 2 tbsp; optional)

4 sheets nori

2 tbsp toasted sesame seeds

1 In a large pan over a medium heat, bring the Dashi Stock to a simmer.

2 Add the ginger, white miso paste, sugar, white soy sauce, soya milk, and salt. Simmer for 10 minutes.

3 Strain the broth, making sure to discard the ginger afterwards.

4 In a large pan of boiling water over a high heat, cook the Ramen Noodles for 50 seconds, stirring occasionally. Drain, rinse, and divide between 4 deep serving bowls.

5 Fill the bowls with the hot broth, just covering the noodles.

6 Neatly arrange the Marinated Soft-Boiled Eggs, spring onions, Menma, and sweetcorn on top of the noodles in each bowl. Place 1 knob of butter (if using) on each pile of sweetcorn.

7 Tuck 1 nori sheet into the broth on the side of each bowl, leaving a corner sticking up. Sprinkle with the toasted sesame seeds.

SHiO DASHi RAMEN WiTH SEAFOOD

In this light, salt-based ramen, the fresh sea flavour of the dashi stock provides a lovely base for the salmon and shrimp. However, feel free to use any seasonal fish or fresh seafood you have to hand.

Prep time 10 mins **Cook time** 15 mins
Yield 4 bowls

1.4l (2½ pints) **Dashi Stock**

2 tbsp sake

1 tbsp mirin

2 tsp sugar

1 tsp white soy sauce

1 tsp sesame oil

1½ tsp sea salt

170g (6oz) fresh shiitake mushrooms, sliced

8–12 medium-large prawns, peeled and deveined

2 x 170g (6oz) salmon fillets, skinless and cut into 2.5cm (1in) chunks

1½ tbsp lemon juice

680g (24oz) fresh **Ramen Noodles**

85g (3oz) spring onions, thinly sliced

85g (3oz) **Menma**

4 sheets nori

2 tbsp toasted sesame seeds

1 In a large pan over a medium heat, bring the Dashi Stock to a simmer.

2 Add the sake, mirin, sugar, white soy sauce, sesame oil, salt, and shiitake mushrooms. Simmer for 10 minutes.

3 Add the prawns, salmon fillets, and lemon juice, and simmer for a further 3 minutes.

4 In a large pan of boiling water over a high heat, cook the Ramen Noodles for 50 seconds, stirring occasionally. Drain, rinse, and divide between 4 deep serving bowls.

5 Fill the bowls with the hot broth, just covering the noodles.

6 Equally divide the prawns and salmon among the bowls. Arrange the spring onions and Menma on top of the noodles in each bowl.

7 Tuck 1 nori sheet into the broth against the side of each bowl. Sprinkle with the toasted sesame seeds.

BACON MiSO DASHi RAMEN

This dish is high on the umami scale! The combination of bacon and dashi is a heavenly marriage of flavours, and the miso and chilli black bean paste bring depth and complexity to the dish.

Prep time 15 mins   **Cook time** 35 mins   **Yield** 4 bowls

3 strips smoked bacon

1.4l (2½ pints) Dashi Stock

2 cloves garlic, crushed

1.25cm (½in) knob ginger, roughly chopped

4 tbsp white miso paste

1 tbsp sugar

1 tbsp soy sauce

2 tsp rice wine vinegar

1½ tsp chilli black bean paste

175g (6oz) firm tofu, diced

2 handfuls spinach

680g (24oz) fresh **Ramen Noodles**

4 **Marinated Soft-Boiled Eggs**, sliced in half lengthways

2 spring onions, finely chopped

1 Cut the smoked bacon in 2.5cm (1in) pieces large enough to fish out of the broth and to fry for the garnish.

2 In a medium pan over a medium heat, simmer the Dashi Stock, garlic, ginger, and bacon for 20 minutes.

3 Strain the broth while reserving pieces of the bacon. Pat dry the bacon with a piece of kitchen paper.

4 Stir in the white miso paste, sugar, soy sauce, rice wine vinegar, and chilli black bean paste. Simmer for 5 minutes.

5 While the broth is simmering, in a medium frying pan over a medium heat, fry the bacon pieces until crispy. Set aside.

6 Add the tofu and spinach to the broth, and simmer for 5 minutes.

7 While the broth is simmering, in a large saucepan of boiling water over a high heat, cook the Ramen Noodles for 50 seconds, stirring occasionally. Drain, rinse, and divide between 4 deep serving bowls.

8 Fill the bowls with the hot broth, just covering the noodles. Top the noodles in each bowl with the bacon pieces, Marinated Soft-Boiled Eggs, and spring onions.

RECiPES WiTH CHiCKEN STOCK

Ramen dishes with a chicken stock base offer a nice medium body and light, clean chicken and vegetable flavours. From green curry, to marsala wine, to lobster egg-drop, you can make a variety of ramen fusion dishes with a chicken stock base.

CHICKEN STOCK

A very popular stock with cooks, chicken stock can be used for a huge variety of bases, from soups to sauces. One of the best things about making your own stock is you have complete control over every ingredient that goes into your pot, allowing you to avoid the salt and preservatives with which canned chicken broth, base, and stock cubes are loaded.

Prep time 10 mins   **Cook time** 5.5 mins
Yield 3l (5 pints)

Ingredients:

2.25kg (5lb) whole chicken

2 large carrots, roughly chopped (no need to peel)

½ cup garlic, crushed

2 bunches spring onions (about 10 stems)

5l (8½ pints) water

1 onion, sliced in half

7.5cm (3in) knob ginger, skin on

Special Equipment:

Fine-mesh skimmer

1 Place the chicken in a large stockpot on the stove. Add the carrots, garlic, and spring onions.

2 Add 4l (7 pints) water to the stockpot, ensuring it covers the chicken with an excess of 5cm (2in) above the chicken.

3 In a large cast-iron pan over a high heat, char the cut side of the onion and ginger until black and fragrant, and then add to the stockpot. You can do this in a dry pan, or over an open gas flame, by holding them over the flame with tongs or setting them on the grate.

4 Bring the stock to the boil, then turn down the heat to a low simmer. Skim any dark foam and matter that floats to the surface with a skimmer for at least the first hour of cooking. During the entire process, the chicken should be fully submerged in water, meaning you may have to periodically top it up with the remaining water. To retain the clarity of the stock, make sure it doesn't boil, but instead stays at a low simmer.

5 Once you have skimmed the chicken stock periodically for the first hour, add the spring onions to the pot.

6 Cook, uncovered, for 2 hours. Carefully remove the chicken, and allow it to cool slightly. Remove the chicken meat, reserving for another use.

Continued

7 Add the chicken bones back to the stock. Bring to the boil over a high heat, and then reduce to a simmer on low. Cook for 3 hours, until the stock has reduced to about 3l (5 pints).

8 Strain the stock and discard the solid bits. The stock is now ready to be used immediately.

Storage: Cool the stock, transfer to a sealable container, and store in the fridge for no more than 1 week. You can also freeze it for up to 6 months.

Chicken Stock

QUICK CHICKEN STOCK

If you're in a hurry and don't have the time to make chicken stock from scratch, cheat with this recipe.

Prep time 10 mins **Cook time** 1.5 hours **Yield** 1.7l (3 pints)

1 Add the chicken breasts, carrot, garlic, onion, ginger, spring onions, and water to a medium-large pot. Bring to the boil over a high heat.

2 Turn down the heat to medium-low, and simmer for 1.5 hours.

3 Strain the stock through a colander, discarding any solids and saving the chicken for another use.

Ingredients:

4 medium chicken breasts

1 large carrot, roughly chopped (no need to peel)

3 cloves garlic, crushed

½ onion, roughly chopped

5cm (2in) knob ginger, skin on

3 spring onions, finely chopped

1.7l (3 pints) water

Storage: The quick chicken stock can be stored in the same way as the regular chicken stock. For easy portions, divide the stock among the compartments in an ice-cube tray, or into 240ml (8fl oz) serving sizes, before freezing.

Quick **Chicken** Stock

THE DiFFERENT PARTS OF CHiCKEN FOR RAMEN

With its succulent, mild flesh that absorbs a variety of flavours, chicken is the most widely eaten meat in the world. One of the cheaper meats you can buy, chicken's not only useful in stock and broth, but also as a tasty topping for your bowl of ramen.

CHOOSiNG CHiCKEN

You can choose from a few different types of chicken to meet your needs.

- Young broilers or roasters have tender meat; older boiling fowl need to be stewed but have excellent flavour.

- Capons are castrated males that are fattened to produce especially tender, plump breasts.

- Free-range, corn-fed, and organic chickens are more expensive than intensively reared, but usually have better flavour and texture.

Drumstick
These make great finger food and are roasted or barbecued plain, marinated, or coated in sauce.

Leg Quarter
Comprising the whole leg plus a part of the backbone and sometimes half the tail, this cut has a moist texture.

Crown
A joint made up of two breasts attached to the breastbone, this is good for those who prefer just the white meat.

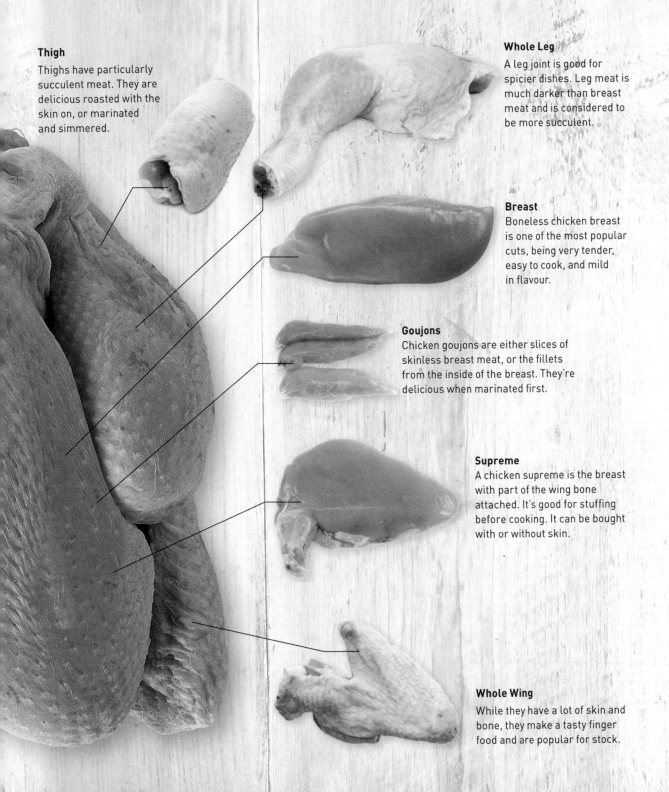

Thigh
Thighs have particularly succulent meat. They are delicious roasted with the skin on, or marinated and simmered.

Whole Leg
A leg joint is good for spicier dishes. Leg meat is much darker than breast meat and is considered to be more succulent.

Breast
Boneless chicken breast is one of the most popular cuts, being very tender, easy to cook, and mild in flavour.

Goujons
Chicken goujons are either slices of skinless breast meat, or the fillets from the inside of the breast. They're delicious when marinated first.

Supreme
A chicken supreme is the breast with part of the wing bone attached. It's good for stuffing before cooking. It can be bought with or without skin.

Whole Wing
While they have a lot of skin and bone, they make a tasty finger food and are popular for stock.

CHICKEN SHOYU RAMEN

You can combine different stocks to create a "double soup". Each stock brings something unique to the table, and by combining two or more, you can add layers of flavour. This light soy-based chicken broth is subtle and nuanced; adding dashi gives the ramen a sea-fresh flavour.

Prep time 20 mins   **Cook time** 20 mins   **Yield** 4 bowls

1l (1¾ pints) **Chicken Stock**

500ml (16fl oz) **Dashi Stock**

5cm (2in) knob ginger, sliced and skin on

4 cloves garlic, crushed

4 tbsp plus 1 tbsp soy sauce

3 tbsp sake

2 tbsp mirin

1½ tsp sugar

680g (24oz) fresh **Ramen Noodles**

350g (12oz) chicken, cooked and shredded

45g (1½oz) spring onions

4 **Marinated Soft-Boiled Eggs**, sliced lengthways

1   In a large pan over a medium heat, bring the Chicken Stock and Dashi Stock to a simmer.

2   Add the ginger, garlic, soy sauce, sake, mirin, and sugar. Simmer for 15 minutes. Strain the broth, discarding any solids.

3   In a large pan of boiling water over a high heat, cook the Ramen Noodles for 50 seconds, stirring occasionally. Drain, rinse, and divide between 4 deep serving bowls.

4   Fill the bowls with the hot broth, just covering the noodles.

5   Neatly arrange the shredded chicken, spring onions, and Marinated Soft-Boiled Eggs on top of the noodles in each bowl.

GiNGER CHiCKEN RAMEN

Just like home-made chicken soup, a bowl of chicken ramen is the ultimate comfort food. Spicy ginger is a prominent flavour in this dish, enhanced by the subtle white soy sauce. Full of flavour, filling, and nourishing, this dish will please the entire family.

Prep time 20 mins **Cook time** 45 mins **Yield** 4 bowls

1l (1¾ pints) **Chicken Stock**

500ml (16fl oz) **Quick Pork Stock**

2 medium boneless, skinless chicken breasts

1 tbsp ginger, finely chopped

2 tsp garlic, finely chopped

80ml (2½fl oz) white soy sauce

3 tbsp mirin

1 tsp sugar

1 tsp sesame oil

2 tsp sea salt (optional)

680g (24oz) fresh **Ramen Noodles**

45g (1½oz) spring onions

4 **Marinated Soft-Boiled Eggs**, sliced in half lengthways

4 sheets nori

45g (1½oz) sesame seeds

1 In a large pan over a medium heat, bring the Chicken Stock and Quick Pork Stock to a simmer.

2 Add the chicken breasts, ginger, garlic, white soy sauce, mirin, sugar, and sesame oil. Simmer for 30–40 minutes, until the chicken is cooked through.

3 Remove the chicken and leave to cool slightly before slicing. Set aside.

4 Taste the broth and season with salt (if using). Turn off the heat just before the noodles are done, then reheat.

5 In a large pan of boiling water over a high heat, cook the Ramen Noodles for 50 seconds, stirring occasionally. Drain, rinse, and divide between 4 deep serving bowls.

6 Fill the bowls with the hot broth, just covering the noodles.

7 Neatly arrange the sliced chicken, spring onions, and Marinated Soft-Boiled Eggs on top of the noodles in each bowl.

8 Tuck 1 nori sheet into the broth against the side of each bowl. Sprinkle with the sesame seeds.

DOUBLE MiSO RAMEN

The salty, fermented complexity of miso makes it a popular seasoning ingredient in Japan. As well as providing a wide variety of health benefits, miso gives depth of flavour to ramen. The addition of dashi stock provides yet another layer of flavour to this dish.

Prep time 10 mins **Cook time** 10 mins **Yield** 4 bowls

1l (1¾ pints) **Chicken Stock**

500ml (16fl oz) **Dashi Stock**

1 tsp sugar

1 tbsp soy sauce

3 tbsp white miso paste

½ tsp sesame oil

175g (6oz) firm tofu, diced

680g (24oz) fresh **Ramen Noodles**

85g (3oz) enoki mushrooms

2 spring onions, thinly sliced

175g (6oz) fresh bean sprouts, blanched

4 **Marinated Soft-Boiled Eggs**, sliced in half lengthways

1 In a large pan over a medium heat, bring the Chicken Stock and Dashi Stock to a simmer.

2 Add the sugar, soy sauce, white miso paste, sesame oil, and tofu. Simmer for 5 minutes.

3 In a large pan of boiling water over a high heat, cook the Ramen Noodles for 50 seconds, stirring occasionally. Drain, rinse, and divide between 4 deep serving bowls.

4 Fill the bowls with the hot broth, just covering the noodles.

5 Neatly arrange the enoki mushrooms, spring onions, bean sprouts, and Marinated Soft-Boiled Eggs on top of the noodles in each bowl.

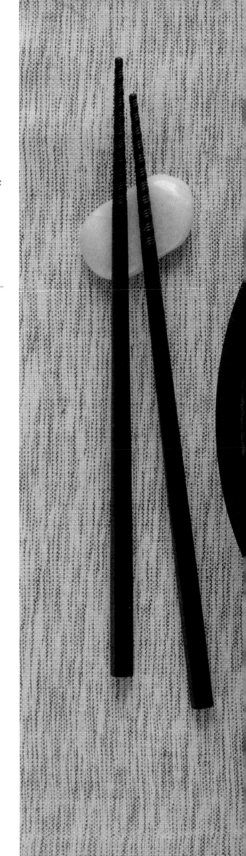

TANTANMEN CHICKEN RAMEN

Packed with heat, this dish features sesame and chilli as the predominant flavours. The pickled vegetables balance the dish with a nice touch of sour.

Prep time 10 mins **Cook time** 20 mins **Yield** 4 bowls

1.4l (2½ pints) **Chicken Stock**

2 tsp ginger, finely chopped

2 tsp garlic, finely chopped

1 tbsp soy sauce

1 tbsp sugar

2 tbsp neri goma or tahini sesame paste

2 tbsp chilli garlic sauce

680g (24oz) fresh **Ramen Noodles**

150g (5½oz) pickled vegetables

8 thin slices **Chashu Pork Loin**, at room temperature

85g (3oz) spring onions, finely chopped

1 tsp sesame oil

1 In a large pan over a medium heat, bring the Chicken Stock, ginger, garlic, soy sauce, sugar, neri goma, and chilli garlic sauce to a simmer.

2 Simmer the broth for 15 minutes, stirring occasionally.

3 In a large pan of boiling water over a high heat, cook the Ramen Noodles for 50 seconds, stirring occasionally. Drain, rinse, and divide between 4 deep serving bowls.

4 Fill the bowls with the hot broth, just covering the noodles.

5 Neatly arrange the pickled vegetables, Chashu Pork Loin, and spring onions on top of the noodles in each bowl. Sprinkle with sesame oil.

KIMCHI APPLE CHICKEN RAMEN WITH BRUSSELS SPROUTS

Pan-fried Brussels sprouts taste fantastic in ramen and are the stars of this dish. The combination of soy and kimchi with the sprouts – along with the more mellow flavours of apple and miso for balance – is definitely a winner!

Prep time 20 mins   **Cook time** 30 mins   **Yield** 4 bowls

1l (1¾ pints) **Chicken Stock**

500ml (16fl oz) **Quick Pork Stock**

140g (5oz) kimchi

1 Granny Smith apple, cored, peeled, and diced

1 tbsp white miso paste

2 tbsp soy sauce

2 tsp sugar

2 tbsp vegetable oil

300g (10oz) Brussels sprouts, trimmed and sliced in half

1 tbsp garlic, finely chopped

2 tbsp reduced-salt soy sauce

680g (24oz) fresh **Ramen Noodles**

1 In a large pan over a medium heat, bring the Chicken Stock and Quick Pork Stock to a simmer.

2 Add the kimchi, Granny Smith apple, white miso paste, soy sauce, and sugar. Simmer for 15 minutes.

3 While the broth is simmering, heat the vegetable oil in a large saucepan over a medium-high heat. Add the Brussels sprouts and garlic to the pan, and cook for 10 minutes, stirring frequently.

4 Add the soy sauce to the sprouts, and cook for 2 more minutes. Turn off the heat and set aside.

5 In a large pan of boiling water over a high heat, cook the Ramen Noodles for 50 seconds, stirring occasionally. Drain, rinse, and divide between 4 deep serving bowls.

6 Fill the bowls with the hot broth, just covering the noodles. Arrange the Brussels sprouts in the middle of each bowl.

SARATANMEN CHiCKEN RAMEN

This sweet-and-sour broth is the perfect way to warm up on a cold day.
Originating in China, this dish has a touch of Chinese black vinegar, which gives
it a unique fruity flavour.

Prep time 25 mins   **Cook time** 30 mins   **Yield** 4 bowls

1.4l (2½ pints) **Chicken Stock**

140g (5oz) carrot, roughly chopped

½ white onion, roughly chopped

5cm (2in) knob ginger, peeled and
sliced

4 shiitake mushrooms, sliced in half

2 tbsp soy sauce

4 tbsp Chinese black vinegar

1 tbsp sake

1 tsp sugar

1 tsp sea salt

180ml (6½fl oz) pineapple juice

2 tsp chilli paste

680g (24oz) fresh **Ramen Noodles**

150g (5½oz) chicken, cooked and
shredded

45g (1½oz) bamboo shoots

2 tbsp coriander, chopped

1 In a large pan over a medium heat, bring the
Chicken Stock to a simmer.

2 Add the carrot, onion, ginger, and shiitake
mushrooms, and simmer for 20 minutes.

3 Add the soy sauce, black vinegar, sake, sugar,
salt, and pineapple juice. Simmer for 5 minutes.
Taste and adjust seasonings as needed.

4 Strain the broth, reserving only the shiitake
mushrooms for garnishing. Discard the
remaining ingredients.

5 Bring the broth back up to a simmer over
a medium heat. Add the chilli paste.

6 In a large pan of boiling water over a high
heat, cook the Ramen Noodles for 50 seconds,
stirring occasionally. Drain, rinse, and divide
between 4 deep serving bowls.

7 Fill the bowls with the hot broth, just covering
the noodles.

8 Garnish each bowl with the chicken, reserved
shiitake mushrooms, bamboo shoots,
and coriander.

MAZEMEN RAMEN WITH TUNA

Mazemen ramen is served with very little broth, converting it to a "dry" style of ramen that showcases the toppings. With so little liquid in the dish, the broth needs to be bold and packed with flavour. The fresh yellowfin tuna steals the show in this dish, providing great texture and picking up flavours from the broth.

Prep time 15 mins   **Cook time** 20 mins   **Yield** 4 bowls

285g (10oz) fresh yellowfin tuna, wrapped in cling film and frozen for 1 hour only

240ml (8fl oz) **Chicken Stock**

180ml (2½fl oz) **Quick Pork Stock**

1 tsp ginger, finely chopped

1 tsp garlic, finely chopped

1 tbsp sake

2 tbsp soy sauce

680g (24oz) fresh **Ramen Noodles**

4 **Marinated Soft-Boiled Eggs**, cut in half lengthways

150g (5½oz) cooked sweetcorn kernels

2 spring onions, finely chopped

2 tbsp sesame seeds

45g (1½oz) nori, finely sliced into ribbons

1 tbsp bonito flakes

1 Remove the tuna from the freezer, take off the cling film, and dice it with a very sharp knife.

2 In a large pan over a medium heat, bring the Chicken Stock and Quick Pork Stock to a simmer.

3 Add the ginger, garlic, sake, and soy sauce. Simmer for 15 minutes.

4 In a large pan of boiling water over a high heat, cook the Ramen Noodles for 50 seconds, stirring occasionally. Drain, rinse, and divide between 4 deep serving bowls.

5 Divide the hot broth between the bowls. The broth won't cover the noodles.

6 Neatly arrange the Marinated Soft-Boiled Eggs, sweetcorn, tuna, and spring onions on top of the noodles in each bowl. Sprinkle with the sesame seeds, nori, and bonito flakes.

Cooked Tuna: Yellowfin tuna is sushi grade and can be eaten raw. if you prefer to cook your tuna, however, you can season it and then sear it in a hot pan with vegetable oil.

SPICY THAI GREEN CURRY RAMEN

This dish combines two delicious foods: ramen and green curry. The green curry paste is a delightful blend of green chillies, galangal, garlic, lemongrass, prawn paste, lime, coriander, and spices. Fragrant and spicy, the recipe is mellowed with a touch of creamy coconut milk. Get ready to be transported to Asia!

Prep time 20 mins   **Cook time** 30 mins   **Yield** 4 bowls

2 medium boneless, skinless chicken breasts

1.4l (2½ pints) **Chicken Stock**

1 tbsp green curry paste

2 tbsp soy sauce

225g (8oz) fresh oyster or shiitake mushrooms, sliced

2–3 small Thai bird's-eye chillies, finely chopped

2 tsp sugar

180ml (6½fl oz) coconut milk

85g (3oz) firm tofu, diced

1 tbsp lime juice

680g (24oz) fresh **Ramen Noodles**

2 tbsp coriander, finely chopped

1 Cut the chicken breasts into 2.5cm (1in) cubes. Set aside.

2 In a large pan over a medium heat, bring the Chicken Stock to a simmer.

3 Add the chicken cubes, green curry paste, soy sauce, oyster mushrooms, Thai bird's-eye chillies, and sugar. Simmer for 20 minutes.

4 Add the coconut milk, tofu, and lime juice, and simmer for a further 5 minutes.

5 In a large pan of boiling water over a high heat, cook the Ramen Noodles for 50 seconds, stirring occasionally. Drain, rinse, and divide between 4 deep serving bowls.

6 Fill the bowls with the hot broth, just covering the noodles.

7 Scoop out equal portions of the chicken into each bowl. Sprinkle the coriander over each bowl.

LOBSTER EGG-DROP RAMEN

This simple Chinese-inspired broth, similar to traditional egg-drop soup, is elevated to gourmet ramen status with the addition of lobster.

Prep time 15 mins   **Cook time** 20 mins
Yield 4 bowls

1.4l (2½ pints) **Chicken Stock**

1 tsp ginger, finely chopped

1 tsp garlic, finely chopped

1 tbsp sake

6 spring onions, finely chopped (reserve some green
  ends for garnish)

1 tbsp fish sauce or white soy sauce

2 tsp sea salt

2 x 140g (5oz) lobster tails

2 eggs

2 tbsp cornflour mixed with 120ml (4fl oz) cold water

680g (24oz) fresh **Ramen Noodles**

150g (5½oz) cooked sweetcorn kernels

4 sheets nori

Special Equipment:

Ice bath

1 In a large pan over a medium heat, bring the Chicken Stock to a simmer.

2 Add the ginger, garlic, sake, spring onions, fish sauce, and salt. Simmer for 5 minutes. Add the lobster tails, and simmer for 5 minutes.

3 While the broth is simmering, in a medium bowl, whisk the eggs. Set aside.

4 Remove the lobster tails from broth, and drop into an ice bath. While the lobster is chilling, add the cornflour mixture to the broth.

5 Bring the broth to the boil, stir, and drizzle in the egg mixture a bit at a time; the mixture will cook immediately. Turn down the heat to low.

6 Remove the meat from the lobster tails, cut in large chunks, and return to the broth.

7 In a large pan of boiling water over a high heat, cook the Ramen Noodles for 50 seconds, stirring occasionally. Drain, rinse, and divide between 4 deep serving bowls.

8 Fill the bowls with the hot broth, just covering the noodles.

9 Equally distribute the lobster meat and sweetcorn between the bowls. Tuck 1 nori sheet into the broth against the side of each bowl.

HOW TO PREPARE LOBSTER

Are you new to cooking lobster? Do you simply have trouble getting all the meat out of it? Never fear! Removing lobster meat is a quick and easy process. Soon enough, you'll have all your yummy lobster meat ready to add to your ramen.

WHOLE LOBSTER

Lobsters are available to buy both live and already prepared. If you'd prefer not to take a live lobster home, the shop will often prepare it for you, but be sure to pick the meat out of the shell that day. When choosing a live lobster, pick one that is lively. It should move its claws and even flap its tail. Limp lobsters should be avoided.

Claw

Tail

Body

Head

PREPARING LOBSTER TAIL

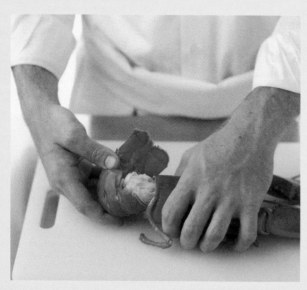

1 Take a firm hold of the tail section and twist sharply to separate it from the body and head section.

2 Turn the lobster tail over, so the underside is face up. Using kitchen scissors, cut down the centre of the shell.

FROZEN LOBSTER TAIL CAUTIONS

When picking out frozen lobster tail for your ramen, you want the freshest and best-quality tails you can find. The following are some common issues to watch out for:

- If possible, choose cold-water tails over warm-water tails. Warm-water tails are more likely to have issues with quality.
- Any lobster tails with a big discount are most likely warm-water tails and therefore lower in quality. Basically, you get what you pay for.
- Discolouration in the flesh, especially black spots, indicates the tails were not handled properly.
- Tails with a greyish colour signify the lobster wasn't alive during processing.
- The meat shouldn't be dull or yellow. Look for white meat.
- Watch for glazing, a process in which water is injected between the meat and the shell before freezing. This can add weight to the tails and lead to higher pricing for less meat.

PREPARING LOBSTER CLAWS

1 With a lobster cracker or a small hammer, crack open the claw shells. Take care not to crush the meat inside.

3 Holding the tail with both hands, press on either side of the cut with your thumbs and pull open the shell. Remove the tail meat in one piece.

2 Remove the meat from the claws, in whole pieces if possible. Discard any membrane attached to the meat.

CHiCKEN MiSO RAMEN

Quick, easy to make, and beautifully satiating, chicken miso ramen is an everyday type of dish. The fermented, salty miso pairs exceptionally well with a chicken stock base, and the white soy sauce adds a delicate depth to the dish.

Prep time 10 mins   **Cook time** 10 mins   **Yield** 4 bowls

1.4l (2½ pints) **Chicken Stock**

45g (1½oz) white miso paste

1 tbsp white soy sauce

2 tsp sake

1 tsp sesame oil

½ tsp sugar

680g (24oz) fresh **Ramen Noodles**

4 **Marinated Soft-Boiled Eggs**, sliced in half lengthways

85g (3oz) spring onions, finely chopped

2 pak choi bulbs, sliced in half lengthways and blanched

150g (5½oz) cooked sweetcorn kernels

1 In a large pan over a medium heat, bring the Chicken Stock to a simmer.

2 Add the white miso paste, white soy sauce, sake, sesame oil, and sugar. Simmer for 5 minutes.

3 In a large pan of boiling water over a high heat, cook the Ramen Noodles for 50 seconds, stirring occasionally. Drain, rinse, and divide between 4 deep serving bowls.

4 Fill the bowls with the hot broth, just covering the noodles.

5 Neatly arrange the Marinated Soft-Boiled Eggs, spring onions, pak choi, and sweetcorn on top of the noodles in each bowl.

CHICKEN SHIO RAMEN

The garlic and ginger really come through with this traditional, clear, salt-based broth. All of the toppings are light, delicate in flavour, and work well with the broth.

Prep time 15 mins   **Cook time** 20 mins   **Yield** 4 bowls

1.4l (2½ pints) **Chicken Stock**

4 garlic cloves, crushed

5cm (2in) knob ginger, sliced

1 tbsp sake

2 tbsp mirin

1½ tsp sea salt

680g (24oz) fresh **Ramen Noodles**

4 **Marinated Soft-Boiled Eggs**, sliced in half lengthways

85g (3oz) spring onions, finely chopped

85g (3oz) **Menma**

150g (5½oz) bean sprouts, blanched

150g (5½oz) beech mushrooms, trimmed

4 sheets nori

1 In a large pan over a medium heat, bring the Chicken Stock, garlic, and ginger to the boil. Reduce heat to low, and simmer for 10 minutes.

2 Strain the broth, discarding the garlic and ginger. Return the broth to the pan and add the sake, mirin, and salt. Simmer for 5 minutes.

3 In a large pan of boiling water over a high heat, cook the Ramen Noodles for 50 seconds, stirring occasionally. Drain, rinse, and divide between 4 deep serving bowls.

4 Fill the bowls with the hot broth, just covering the noodles.

5 Neatly arrange the spring onions, Menma, bean sprouts, and beech mushrooms on top of the noodles in each bowl.

6 Tuck 1 nori sheet into the broth on the side of each bowl, leaving a corner sticking up over the top of the bowl.

BUTTER SWEEETCORN CHiCKEN RAMEN

Rich, hearty, and utterly delicious, this ramen is perfect when the nights start to become a little chilly. Make this ramen in late summer, when fresh sweetcorn is at its sweetest. The contrast of the sweet corn and salty miso is a real winner.

Prep time 15 mins   **Cook time** 20 mins   **Yield** 4 bowls

1.4l (2½ pints) **Chicken Stock**

1 tbsp garlic, finely chopped

1 tbsp shallots, finely chopped

45g (1½oz) white miso paste

1½ tsp sugar

8 slices **Chasu Pork Belly**

1 tsp sea salt

680g (24oz) fresh **Ramen Noodles**

4 **Marinated Soft-Boiled Eggs**, sliced in half lengthways

85g (3oz) spring onions, finely chopped

300g (10oz) cooked sweetcorn kernels

4 small knobs butter (about 2 tbsp)

45g (1½oz) sesame seeds

1 In a large pan over a medium heat, bring the Chicken Stock to a simmer.

2 Add the garlic, shallots, white miso paste, and sugar. Simmer for 10 minutes.

3 While the broth is simmering, heat a large frying pan over high heat.

4 Sprinkle the Chashu Pork Belly with the salt, add to frying pan, and sear on both sides for 2 minutes each.

5 In a large pan of boiling water over a high heat, cook the Ramen Noodles for 50 seconds, stirring occasionally. Drain, rinse, and divide between 4 deep serving bowls.

6 Fill the bowls with the hot broth, just covering the noodles.

7 Neatly arrange the Marinated Soft-Boiled Eggs, Chashu Pork Belly, spring onions, and sweetcorn on top of the noodles.

8 Place 1 knob butter on each pile of sweetcorn. Sprinkle the sesame seeds over the bowls.

PEANUT CHICKEN SATAY RAMEN

Inspired by chicken satay, this ramen has a rich broth flavoured with peanut butter and curry.

Prep time 4.5 hours **Cook time** 35 mins
Yield 4 bowls

2 medium fresh chicken breasts

4 tbsp plus 1½ tbsp soy sauce

2 garlic cloves, finely chopped

1 tsp grated ginger

1 tbsp light brown sugar

2 tbsp lime juice

1 tsp plus 1 tbsp curry powder

1 tbsp vegetable oil

1 tbsp garlic, finely chopped

1 tbsp ginger, finely chopped

1 tbsp sugar

1.4l (2½ pints) **Chicken Stock**

150g (5½oz) finely chopped tomatoes

140g (5oz) peanut butter

180ml (6½fl oz) coconut milk

2 tsp crushed chilli flakes

1 tsp sea salt

680g (24oz) fresh **Ramen Noodles**

4 **Marinated Soft-Boiled Eggs**

85g (3oz) cooked sweetcorn

1 red pepper, thinly sliced

45g (1½oz) coriander

4 lime wedges

Special Equipment:

8 bamboo skewers

Grill

1 Pat the chicken breasts dry with kitchen paper. Cut the chicken into strips approximately 7.5–12.5cm (3–5in) long and 2.5cm (1in) wide.

2 Prepare the marinade. In a large bowl, mix 4 tablespoons soy sauce, garlic, grated ginger, light brown sugar, lime juice, and 1 teaspoon curry powder. Place the chicken strips in the marinade. Refrigerate for 2–4 hours.

3 Soak the bamboo skewers in cold water for 20 minutes so they don't burn when on the grill.

4 Take the chicken strips out of the marinade and divide among the bamboo skewers. Set aside.

5 Prepare the broth. Heat the vegetable oil in a large pan over a medium-high heat. Add the garlic, ginger, sugar, and remaining 1 tablespoon curry powder. Cook for 1 minute, stirring constantly.

6 Add the Chicken Stock, tomatoes, peanut butter, remaining 1½ tablespoons soy sauce, coconut milk, crushed chilli flakes, and salt, and bring to the boil. Reduce the heat, and simmer for 15 minutes.

7 Grill the chicken skewers for approximately 5 minutes on each side, depending on the thickness. Set aside.

8 In a large saucepan of boiling water over a high heat, cook the Ramen Noodles for 50 seconds, stirring occasionally. Drain, rinse, and divide between 4 deep serving bowls.

9 Fill the bowls with the hot broth, just covering the noodles.

10 Arrange 2 skewers of chicken in each bowl, as well as the Marinated Soft-Boiled Eggs, sweetcorn, red pepper, and coriander. Serve with the lime wedges.

CHICKEN MARSALA RAMEN

Italian and Japanese cuisines share a similar love of pasta and noodles, so why not marry some of the flavours? Mushrooms and marsala wine complement each other perfectly and give an Italian feel to this ramen dish.

Prep time 15 mins   **Cook time** 35 mins   **Yield** 4 bowls

2 tbsp butter

150g (5½oz) fresh shiitake mushrooms, sliced

150g (5½oz) fresh oyster mushrooms, sliced

1 tbsp garlic, finely chopped

2 tbsp shallots, finely chopped

1 tbsp fresh thyme, pulled from stem and finely chopped

240ml (8fl oz) dry marsala wine

1l (1¾ pints) **Chicken Stock**

500ml (16fl oz) **Tonkotsu Pork Stock**

2 tsp sea salt

120ml (4fl oz) lemon juice

1 tsp sugar

680g (24oz) fresh **Ramen Noodles**

4 **Soft-Boiled Eggs**, sliced in half lengthways

150g (5½oz) cooked chicken, shredded

2 tbsp spring onions, finely chopped

1 In a large pan over a medium-high heat, melt the butter. Add the shiitake and oyster mushrooms, and cook for 5 minutes, stirring occasionally.

2 Add the garlic, shallots, and thyme. Cook for 3 minutes, stirring constantly, until the juices have evaporated.

3 Add the marsala wine to the pan, and deglaze by scraping up any bits on the bottom. Cook for 5 minutes, or until the liquid is reduced by half.

4 Add the Chicken Stock and Tonkotsu Pork Stock, and bring to the boil over a high heat.

5 Reduce to a simmer over a low heat and add the salt, lemon juice, and sugar. Simmer for 10 minutes. Taste and adjust seasonings, if necessary.

6 In a large pan of boiling water over a high heat, cook the Ramen Noodles for 50 seconds, stirring occasionally. Drain, rinse, and divide between 4 deep serving bowls.

7 Fill the bowls with the hot broth, just covering the noodles. Neatly arrange the Soft-Boiled Eggs, chicken, and spring onions on top of the noodles in each bowl.

RECiPES WiTH PORK STOCK

You'll find you can build hundreds of variations of ramen with rich, creamy tonkotsu pork stock or quick pork stock. From pairing tonkotsu stock with the sea flavours of bonito, to creating a pork red curry ramen, the possibilities are endless!

TONKOTSU PORK STOCK

Making your own pork stock is an incredibly rewarding labour of love. During the cooking process, you'll see the stock go from clear to milky-white, due to the break down of collagen in the pork bones being absorbed into the stock. The stock isn't seasoned, which will give you the freedom to season your ramen according to each recipe.

Prep time 45 mins   **Cook time** 12 hours
Yield 2–3l (3½–5¼ pints)

Ingredients:

4 pig trotters (ask your butcher to cut them in quarters)

2–4 smoked hocks (optional)

1kg (2lb) pork thigh bones

1kg (2lb) chicken bones

450g (1lb) pork back fat

2 onions, sliced in half and ends removed

7.5cm (3in) knob ginger, skin on

4 leeks, roughly chopped and cleaned

2 large carrots, roughly chopped (no need to peel)

170g (6oz) garlic, crushed

3 bunches spring onions (about 15–20 stems), ends removed

2 Granny Smith apples, quartered

Special Equipment:

Large colander and cheesecloth

Chopstick or knife

Fine-mesh skimmer

1 Place the pig trotters, smoked hocks (if using), pork thigh bones, chicken bones, and pork back fat in a large stockpot, and cover with water. Leave to sit for at least 1 hour to help remove blood and impurities.

2 Strain the bones into a large colander, and discard the water. Place the bones back in the pot and add fresh water, just covering the bones.

3 Place the pot on the hob over a high heat. Just before the water boils, remove the pot and drain the bones in the colander again. Rinse each bone under the tap, ensuring you remove all of the blood and dark matter. Use a chopstick or knife for this purpose.

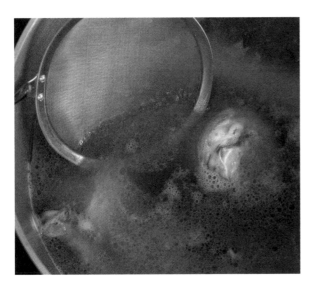

4 Once clean, return the bones to the pot and add at least 4l (7 pints) water, ensuring the bones are submerged. Bring to the boil over a high heat. Skim the stock with a skimmer for at least 30 minutes to remove any grey scum. Place a fitted lid on the pot, and boil for 6 hours.

5 In a large pan over a high heat, char the cut side of the onions and ginger until black and fragrant.

Continued

6 Add the charred onions and ginger, leeks, carrots, garlic, spring onions, and Granny Smith apple quarters to the stock. Simmer briskly for 5 hours. Stir the bones every 45 minutes to ensure they don't brown.

7 Strain the stock using a fine-mesh strainer, or a colander with a cheesecloth, and discard the solid bits. The stock is ready to be used immediately.

Storage: Allow the stock to cool, and then transfer it to a sealable container. You can store it in the fridge for no more than 1 week or in the freezer for up to 6 months.

Pork Stock

QUiCK PORK STOCK

This quick stock is clear and light, but will still provide a lovely pork-flavoured base for your ramen soups. Like the previous pork stock recipe, the stock isn't seasoned, which will give you the freedom to season your ramen according to each recipe.

Prep time 20 mins   **Cook time** 2.5 hours   **Yield** 2–3l (3½–5¼ pints)

1 Place the pork bones in a large stockpot, cover with cold water, and bring to the boil over a high heat. Just before the water boils, drain the bones in a colander, rinse them, and return them to a cleaned pot. Add at least 2l (3½ pints) fresh water.

2 In a dry pan over a high heat, char the onions and ginger. Add the charred onions and ginger, carrots, garlic, spring onions, and tart apples to the pot.

3 Place the pot on the hob over high heat, and bring to the boil. Reduce to a simmer and cook for 2 hours.

4 Strain the stock and discard the solid bits. The stock is ready to be used immediately.

Storage: Store this stock in the same way as the primary pork stock. if freezing, freeze in individual portions or ice-cube trays for easy use.

Ingredients:

1.5kg (3lb) pork bones

2 onions, roughly chopped

5cm (2in) knob ginger, sliced

2 large carrots, roughly chopped (no need to peel)

85g (3oz) garlic, crushed

1 bunch spring onions (5–10 stems), roughly chopped

2 tart apples (such as Granny Smith), quartered

Special Equipment:

Large colander

Skimmer

Quick **Pork** Stock

BARBECUE PORK TSUKEMEN

Inspired by traditional American barbecue dishes, this dipping ramen has a smoky barbecue flavour accompanied by two favourite barbecue sides – sweetcorn and greens!

Prep time 15 mins **Cook time** 25 mins **Yield** 4 bowls

680g (24oz) fresh **Ramen Noodles**

750ml (1¼ pints) **Quick Pork Stock**

1½ tbsp mirin

3 tbsp soy sauce

4 tbsp barbecue sauce

1½ tsp black vinegar

¾ tsp crushed chilli flakes

4 spring onions, finely chopped

2 tsp sea salt

1 tbsp lemon juice

1 bunch (about 5 stems) mustard greens, stemmed and chopped

1 tbsp vegetable oil

12 slices **Chashu Pork Belly**

4 **Marinated Soft-Boiled Eggs**, halved lengthways

150g (5½oz) cooked sweetcorn kernels

85g (3oz) **Menma**

Special Equipment:

8 serving dishes or bamboo mats

1 In a large pan of boiling water over a high heat, cook the Ramen Noodles for 50 seconds, stirring occasionally. Drain, rinse, and divide between 4 serving dishes or bamboo mats.

2 Heat the Quick Pork Stock in another large pan over a medium heat. Add the mirin, soy sauce, barbecue sauce, black vinegar, crushed chilli flakes, and spring onions. Simmer for 10 minutes.

3 In a medium pan over a high heat, boil 1.2l (5 cups) water, 1 teaspoon salt, and the lemon juice. Once the water is boiling, add the mustard greens, and cook for 5 minutes. Drain and set aside.

4 Heat the vegetable oil in a large frying pan over a medium-high heat. Sprinkle the remaining salt over the Chashu Pork Belly. Sear it in the pan on both sides, about 2 minutes on each side. Remove from the pan and set aside.

5 Fill 4 deep serving bowls with the broth. Divide the Chashu Pork Belly, Marinated Soft-Boiled Eggs, sweetcorn, mustard greens, and Menma between 4 serving dishes or bamboo mats.

6 Serve each guest a bowl of broth, a dish of noodles, and a dish of garnishes.

SPICY MISO PORK RAMEN

Packed with umami, this hearty dish offers up a pleasing bowl of ground pork, pungent red miso paste, and fiery chilli flakes. Chilli black bean paste – a medium-hot mixture of black beans, chilli, vinegar, and sesame oil – provides a spicy tang to the dish and complements the pork.

Prep time 15 mins   **Cook time** 25 mins
Yield 4 bowls

1.4l (2½ pints) **Quick Pork Stock**

3 tbsp chilli black bean paste

2 tsp rice wine vinegar

1 tbsp sugar

3 tbsp red miso paste

2 tbsp vegetable oil

1 tbsp garlic, finely chopped

225g (8oz) minced pork

2 tbsp soy sauce

1 tsp crushed chilli flakes

680g (24oz) fresh **Ramen Noodles**

4 **Marinated Soft-Boiled Eggs**, sliced in half lengthways

85g (3oz) cooked sweetcorn kernels

2 spring onions, finely chopped

2 tsp **Burnt Garlic Oil**

4 sheets nori

1 In a large pan over a medium heat, bring the Quick Pork Stock to a simmer.

2 Add the chilli black bean paste, rice wine vinegar, sugar, and red miso paste. Simmer for 10 minutes.

3 While the broth is simmering, heat a large frying pan over a medium-high heat, and add the vegetable oil.

4 Add the garlic and pork to the pan, and cook until the meat begins to brown, about 3–5 minutes.

5 Add the soy sauce and crushed chilli flakes to the pork mixture, and cook for 3 minutes or until cooked through. Turn off the heat and set aside.

6 In a large pan of boiling water over a high heat, cook the Ramen Noodles for 50 seconds, stirring occasionally. Drain, rinse, and divide between 4 deep serving bowls.

7 Fill the bowls with the hot broth, just covering the noodles.

8 Arrange the pork, Marinated Soft-Boiled Eggs, sweetcorn, and spring onions on top of the noodles in each bowl.

9 Drizzle the Burnt Garlic Oil over each bowl. Arrange 1 nori sheet along the side of each bowl, halfway in broth.

BONITO PORK RAMEN

Bonito flakes, a staple in Japanese cooking, lend a savoury, salty flavour to this pork-based ramen. This land-and-sea combination of bonito and pork creates a dish that's simple and delicious.

Prep time 20 mins   **Cook time** 20 mins   **Yield** 4 bowls

1.4l (2½ pints) **Tonkotsu Pork Stock**

4 tsp soy sauce

2 tsp sea salt

1 tbsp mirin

1 tbsp sake

30g (1oz) bonito flakes, tightly packed

8 slices **Chashu Pork Belly**

1 tbsp vegetable oil

680g (24oz) fresh **Ramen Noodles**

85g (3oz) fresh radishes, thinly sliced

85g (3oz) beech mushrooms, trimmed

45g (1½oz) spring onion greens, thinly sliced

4 sheets nori

1 In a large pan over a medium heat, bring the Tonkotsu Pork Stock to a simmer.

2 Add the soy sauce, 1 teaspoon salt, the mirin, sake, and bonito flakes. Simmer for 10 minutes.

3 In the meantime, heat the vegetable oil in a large frying pan over a medium-high heat. Sprinkle the remaining salt over the Chashu Pork Belly. Sear in the pan on both sides until golden, about 2 minutes for each side. Remove from the pan and set aside.

4 In a large pan of boiling water over a high heat, cook the Ramen Noodles for 50 seconds, stirring occasionally. Drain, rinse, and divide between 4 deep serving bowls.

5 Strain the broth, discarding the bonito flakes. Pour the hot broth into each of the serving bowls, just covering the noodles.

6 Neatly arrange the Chashu Pork Belly, radishes, beech mushrooms, and spring onions on top of the noodles in each bowl. Arrange 1 nori sheet along the side of each bowl, halfway in the broth.

SWEET-AND-SOUR SPICY PORK RAMEN

Borrowed from the Chinese, this dish has pineapple juice, which gives the broth its sweet-and-sour flavour, as well as fiery chilli garlic sauce.

Prep time 15 mins **Cook time** 25 mins **Yield** 4 bowls

1.4l (2½ pints) **Quick Pork Stock**

6 tbsp red miso paste

1½ tsp Chinese black vinegar

1 tbsp chilli garlic sauce

1 tbsp sugar

120ml (4fl oz) pineapple juice

1 tbsp vegetable oil

225g (8oz) minced pork

1 tbsp garlic, finely chopped

2 tbsp soy sauce

1 tsp crushed chilli flakes

680g (24oz) fresh **Ramen Noodles**

85g (3oz) **Menma**

4 **Marinated Soft-Boiled Eggs**, sliced in half lengthways

85g (3oz) spring onions, finely chopped

4 sheets nori

1 In a large pan over a medium heat, bring the Quick Pork Stock to a simmer.

2 Add the red miso paste, black vinegar, chilli garlic sauce, sugar, and pineapple juice. Simmer for 10 minutes.

3 While the broth is simmering, heat the vegetable oil in a large frying pan over a medium-high heat.

4 Add the pork and garlic to the pan. Cook until the meat begins to brown, about 6 to 8 minutes.

5 Add the soy sauce and crushed chilli flakes, and cook for 3 minutes, until cooked through. Turn off the heat and set aside.

6 In a large pan of boiling water over a high heat, cook the Ramen Noodles for 50 seconds, stirring occasionally. Drain, rinse, and divide between 4 deep serving bowls.

7 Fill the bowls with the hot broth, just covering the noodles. Add the cooked pork to each bowl.

8 Neatly arrange the Menma, Marinated Soft-Boiled Eggs, and spring onions on top of the noodles in each bowl. Arrange 1 nori sheet along the side of each bowl, halfway in the broth.

TONKOTSU RAMEN

One of the most famous and well-loved ramen varieties, tonkotsu is rich, silky, complex, and extremely satisfying.

Prep time 20 mins   **Cook time** 15 mins   **Yield** 4 bowls

1.4l (2½ pints) **Tonkotsu Pork Stock**

1 tbsp sake

2½ tsp sea salt

½ tsp sriracha

2 tsp mirin

½ tsp sugar

1 tbsp vegetable oil

8 slices **Chashu Pork Belly**

680g (24oz) fresh **Ramen Noodles**

4 **Marinated Soft-Boiled Eggs**, room temperature and sliced in half lengthways

4 slices narutomaki (fish cake)

45g (1½oz) spring onions, finely chopped

4 sheets nori

1 In a large pan over a medium heat, bring the Tonkotsu Pork Stock to a simmer.

2 Add the sake, 2 teaspoons salt, sriracha, mirin, and sugar. Simmer for 10 minutes. (Tip: If desired, you may use the braising liquid from the Chashu Pork Belly to season this ramen. Add 2 tablespoons at a time until you achieve your desired level of flavour and saltiness.)

3 While the broth is simmering, heat a large non-stick pan over a medium-high heat. Add the vegetable oil.

4 Season the slices of Chashu Pork Belly with the remaining salt, then add to the pan.

5 Sear on both sides until golden brown, about 2 minutes on each side. Set the Chashu Pork Belly aside.

6 In a large pan of boiling water over a high heat, cook the Ramen Noodles for 50 seconds, stirring occasionally. Drain, rinse, and divide between 4 deep serving bowls.

7 Fill the bowls with the hot broth, just covering the noodles.

8 Neatly arrange the Chashu Pork Belly, Marinated Soft-Boiled Eggs, narutomaki, spring onions, and nori on top of the noodles in each bowl.

PORK SHIO RAMEN

This dish is a lighter version of tonkotsu ramen made with the Quick Pork Stock. As the title implies, this ramen is salt based. The addition of chicken stock gives it an added complexity in the flavour profile.

Prep time 20 mins   **Cook time** 20 mins   **Yield** 4 bowls

1l (1¾ pints) **Quick Pork Stock**

500ml (16fl oz) **Chicken Stock**

3 tbsp white soy sauce

1 tbsp sea salt

3 tbsp mirin

2 tsp sugar

1 tsp rice wine vinegar

140g (5oz) fresh shiitake mushrooms, sliced

680g (24oz) fresh **Ramen Noodles**

85g (3oz) sliced pickled radish

8 slices **Chashu Pork Loin**

4 **Marinated Soft-Boiled Eggs**, sliced in half lengthways

85g (3oz) spring onions, finely chopped

4 sheets nori

1 In a large pan over a medium heat, bring the Quick Pork Stock and Chicken Stock to a simmer.

2 Add the white soy sauce, salt, mirin, sugar, rice wine vinegar, and shiitake mushrooms. Simmer for 15 minutes.

3 In a large pan of boiling water over a high heat, cook the Ramen Noodles for 50 seconds, stirring occasionally. Drain, rinse, and divide between 4 deep serving bowls.

4 Fill the bowls with the hot broth, just covering the noodles.

5 Neatly arrange the pickled radish, Chashu Pork Loin, Marinated Soft-Boiled Eggs, and spring onions on top of the noodles in each bowl. Arrange 1 nori sheet along the side of each bowl, halfway in the broth.

BACON AND PICKLED APPLE TONKOTSU RAMEN

Pork and apples are a classic flavour combination in the West, with the sweet, tart apples perfectly balancing the fatty, rich tonkotsu broth. The bacon gives the broth an extra-smoky flavour.

Prep time 1 hour   **Cook time** 30 mins
Yield 4 bowls

240ml (8fl oz) water
120ml (4fl oz) rice wine vinegar
50g (1¾oz) plus 1 tsp sugar
50g (1¾oz) plus 1 tbsp mirin
2½ tsp sea salt
10cm (4in) strip kombu (kelp)
1 Granny Smith apple, peeled and thinly sliced
1.4l (2½ pints) **Tonkotsu Pork Stock**
5 rashers thick smoked bacon, roughly chopped
1½ tbsp white soy sauce
1 tbsp vegetable oil
680g (24oz) fresh Ramen Noodles
8 slices **Chashu Pork Loin,** very thinly sliced
4 **Marinated Soft-Boiled Eggs,** sliced in half lengthways
85g (3oz) spring onion greens, finely chopped
4 sheets nori

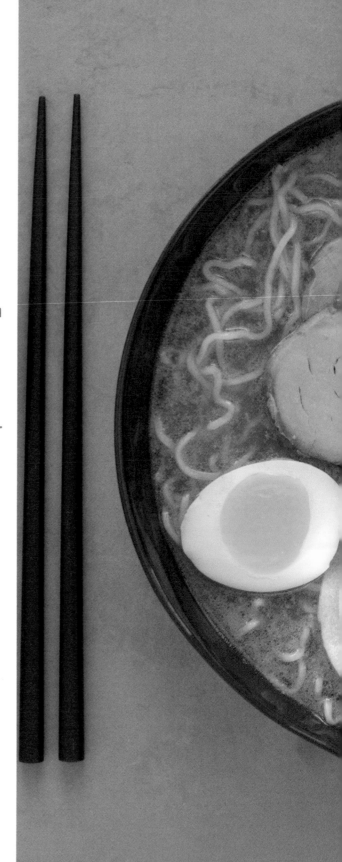

1 In a small pan, combine the water, rice wine vinegar, 50g (¼ cup) sugar, 50g (¼ cup) mirin, 1 teaspoon salt, and the kombu. Bring to the boil over a high heat.

2 Once the mixture reaches boiling point, turn off the heat and add the Granny Smith apple slices. Set aside for 30 minutes.

3 In a large pan over a medium heat, bring the Tonkotsu Pork Stock and bacon to a simmer.

4 Add the white soy sauce, remaining salt, remaining mirin, and remaining sugar to the pan. Simmer for 10 minutes.

5 Strain the broth, reserving the pieces of bacon. Set aside.

6 Strain the Granny Smith apple slices from the pickling liquid and set aside. Discard the liquid.

7 Pat the bacon dry. In a medium frying pan over a medium-high heat, add the vegetable oil. Add the bacon pieces, and fry until crispy. Set aside.

8 In a large pan of boiling water over a high heat, cook the Ramen Noodles for 50 seconds, stirring occasionally. Drain, rinse, and divide between 4 deep serving bowls.

9 Fill the bowls with the hot broth, just covering the noodles.

10 Neatly arrange the Chashu Pork Loin, Granny Smith apple slices, Marinated Soft-Boiled Eggs, spring onions, and bacon pieces on top of the noodles in each bowl.

11 Arrange 1 nori sheet along the side of each bowl, halfway in the broth.

CUBAN PORK RAMEN

This dish borrows the flavour profile of the popular Cuban sandwich, which combines pork, Swiss cheese, and pickled vegetables. Adding Dijon mustard to the broth gives it a little kick that works really well with the pork.

Prep time 20 mins   **Cook time** 15 mins   **Yield** 4 bowls

1.4l (2½ pints) **Tonkotsu Pork Stock**

2½ tbsp Dijon mustard

2½ tbsp soy sauce

1½ tbsp mirin

680g (24oz) fresh **Ramen Noodles**

8 slices **Chashu Pork Loin**, thinly sliced

140g (5oz) pickled vegetables

45g (1½oz) spring onion greens, thinly sliced

85g (3oz) Swiss cheese, shredded

1 In a large pan over a medium heat, bring the Tonkotsu Pork Stock to a simmer.

2 Add the Dijon mustard, soy sauce, and mirin. Simmer for 5 minutes.

3 In a large pan of boiling water over a high heat, cook the Ramen Noodles for 50 seconds, stirring occasionally. Drain, rinse, and divide between 4 deep serving bowls.

4 Fill the bowls with the hot broth, just covering the noodles.

5 Neatly arrange the Chashu Pork Loin, pickled vegetables, spring onions, and Swiss cheese on top of the noodles in each bowl.

CHINESE SAUSAGE AND SCALLOP PORK RAMEN

This is a hearty ramen packed with flavour. Chinese sausage has a lovely sweet pork taste that works well with the mild, creamy scallops.

Prep time 20 mins   **Cook time** 20 mins   **Yield** 4 bowls

1 tbsp vegetable oil

1 tbsp shallots, finely chopped

350g (12oz) Chinese sausage, sliced 5mm (¼in) thick

1 tbsp garlic, finely chopped

1l (1¾ pints) **Quick Pork Stock**

500ml (16fl oz) **Chicken Stock**

1½ tbsp soy sauce

2 tsp sake

2 tsp Chinese black vinegar

2 tsp sugar

1 tsp sea salt

175g (6oz) fresh hen-of-the-woods mushrooms, sliced

285g (10oz) bay scallops

175g (6oz) spinach

680g (24oz) fresh **Ramen Noodles**

85g (3oz) spring onions, finely chopped

4 sheets nori

1 Heat the vegetable oil in a large pan over a medium heat. Add the shallots, and cook for 1 minute.

2 Add the Chinese sausage, and sauté for 2 minutes. Add the garlic, and cook for 1 minute.

3 Add the Quick Pork Stock, Chicken Stock, soy sauce, sake, black vinegar, sugar, salt, and hen-of-the-woods mushrooms. Simmer for 10 minutes.

4 Add the bay scallops and spinach. Simmer for 2 minutes, or until the scallops have cooked through and are firm to the touch.

5 In a large pan of boiling water over a high heat, cook the Ramen Noodles for 50 seconds, stirring occasionally. Drain, rinse, and divide between 4 deep serving bowls.

6 Fill the bowls with the hot broth, just covering the noodles.

7 Evenly divide the scallops between the bowls. Sprinkle the spring onions on top of the noodles in each bowl. Arrange 1 nori sheet along the side of each bowl, halfway in the broth.

GEKIKARA (SPICY) RAMEN

Gekikara is a spicy ramen packed with flavour. The addition of the chilli garlic sauce, along with chilli flakes, gives the dish a unique kick. The sautéed leeks balance the heat well and provide a good texture contrast.

Prep time 15 mins   **Cook time** 35 mins   **Yield** 4 bowls

2 bunches leeks (about 6)

1 tbsp vegetable oil

1 tbsp butter

1 tsp sea salt

1.4l (2½ pints) **Tonkotsu Pork Stock**

1 tbsp sake

1 tbsp chilli garlic sauce

1 tsp crushed chilli flakes

680g (24oz) fresh **Ramen Noodles**

4 **Soft-Boiled Eggs**, sliced in half lengthways

175g (6oz) cooked sweetcorn kernels

85g (3oz) spring onions, finely chopped

45g (1½oz) toasted sesame seeds

1 Thinly slice the leeks into rings, keeping only the white and light-coloured green parts. Wash thoroughly in a colander. Drain well.

2 Heat the vegetable oil and butter in a large pan over a medium heat.

3 Add the leeks and salt, and sauté for 20 minutes, stirring frequently, until the leeks begin to caramelize.

4 Add the Tonkotsu Pork Stock, sake, chilli garlic sauce, and crushed chilli flakes. Simmer for 10 minutes. Taste and adjust seasonings, if necessary.

5 In a large pan of boiling water over a high heat, cook the Ramen Noodles for 50 seconds, stirring occasionally. Drain, rinse, and divide between 4 deep serving bowls.

6 Fill the bowls with the hot broth, just covering the noodles.

7 Neatly arrange the Soft-Boiled Eggs, sweetcorn, and spring onions on top of the noodles in each bowl. Sprinkle the toasted sesame seeds over the bowls.

PORK RED CURRY RAMEN

Fragrant and bold, this curry dish is flavoured with Thai red curry paste and Indian curry powder. The lime juice highlights the curry, and the fish sauce gives the dish depth.

Prep time 15 mins   **Cook time** 15 mins
Yield 4 bowls

1 tbsp vegetable oil

1 tbsp grated ginger

1 tbsp garlic, crushed

3 tbsp Thai red curry paste

2 tsp medium curry
   powder

1.4l (2½ pints) **Quick Pork
   Stock**

1½ tbsp fish sauce

390ml can coconut milk

1½ tbsp light brown sugar

1½ tsp sea salt

2 tbsp lime juice

175g (6oz) spinach

680g (24oz) fresh
   Ramen Noodles

285g (10oz) **Chashu Pork
   Loin**, thinly sliced

45g (1½oz) spring onions

45g (1½oz) coriander,
   roughly chopped

4 lime wedges

1 Heat the vegetable oil in a large pan over a medium heat. Add the ginger, garlic, Thai red curry paste, and curry powder. Cook for 1 minute, stirring constantly.

2 Add the Quick Pork Stock, and simmer for 5 minutes.

3 Add the fish sauce, coconut milk, sugar, salt, and lime juice. Simmer on a low heat for 5 minutes. Taste and adjust seasonings, if necessary.

4 Divide the spinach between 4 deep serving bowls.

5 In a large pan of boiling water over a high heat, cook the Ramen Noodles for 50 seconds, stirring occasionally. Drain, rinse, and divide between the 4 bowls.

6 Fill the bowls with the hot broth, just covering the noodles.

7 Neatly arrange the Chashu Pork Loin and spring onions on top of the noodles in each bowl. Sprinkle the coriander on top, and serve with lime wedges.

RECiPES WiTH VEGETARiAN STOCK

Ramen can and should be enjoyed by vegetarians!
Light, fresh, and fragrant, vegetarian stock is a
great base for many different types of meat-free
ramen dishes, such as tomato miso, curried
tofu, and sweetcorn chowder.

VEGETARIAN STOCK

This vegetarian stock is light and fragrant, and will provide a good alternative to meat-based stock. Vegetarian stock pairs very well with miso, mushrooms, tomatoes, and sweetcorn. Charring the onion and ginger will increase their flavour profiles. Do it over an open flame or in a dry pan over a high heat.

Prep time 15 mins–overnight   **Cook time** 45 mins
Yield 1.4–1.7l (2½–3 pints)

Ingredients:

2 tbsp vegetable oil

1 large onion, roughly chopped

2 celery stalks, roughly chopped

5cm (2in) knob ginger, sliced

2 leeks, sliced and washed

2 large carrots, roughly chopped (no need to peel)

85g (3oz) garlic, finely chopped

2l (3½ pints) water

175g (6oz) button mushrooms, roughly chopped

1 bunch spring onions (6–8 stems), roughly chopped

1 Heat the vegetable oil in a large pot over a medium-high heat. Add the onion, celery, ginger, leeks, carrots, and garlic.

2 Stirring constantly, cook for 10 minutes to caramelize the vegetables.

3 Add the water and bring to the boil over a high heat. Add the button mushrooms and spring onions, lower the heat to a simmer, and cook for 30 minutes.

4 Allow to cool until it's room temperature, or overnight in the fridge to allow maximum infused flavour. Strain the stock and discard the solids.

Storage: Allow the stock to cool, then transfer it to a sealable container. You can store it in the fridge for no more than 1 week. This stock also freezes well in an ice-cube tray or 240ml (8fl oz) portions for up to 6 months.

Vegetarian Stock

MUSHROOM MiSO VEGETARIAN RAMEN

A light, miso-based soup, this ramen will appeal to mushroom lovers, as it contains three different types. The mushrooms bring an earthy flavour to the ramen, which pairs very well with both the tofu and miso.

Prep time 10 mins   **Cook time** 30 mins   **Yield** 4 bowls

1.4l (2½ pints) **Vegetarian Stock**

85g (3oz) oyster mushrooms, sliced

85g (3oz) shiitake mushrooms

8 spring onions, finely chopped (reserve some green for garnish)

4 tbsp vegetarian white miso paste

175g (6oz) firm tofu, diced

85g (3oz) baby spinach

680g (24oz) fresh **Ramen Noodles**

175g (6oz) fresh enoki mushrooms, trimmed

4 sheets nori, sliced into strips

1 In a large pan over a medium heat, bring the Vegetarian Stock to a simmer.

2 Add the oyster mushrooms, shiitake mushrooms, and spring onions, and simmer for 20 minutes.

3 Add the vegetarian white miso paste, tofu, and baby spinach. Simmer for 5 minutes.

4 While the broth is simmering, in a large pan of boiling water over a high heat, cook the Ramen Noodles for 50 seconds, stirring occasionally. Drain, rinse, and divide between 4 deep serving bowls.

5 Fill the bowls with the hot broth, just covering the noodles.

6 Add the enoki mushrooms and nori strips to each bowl.

TOM YUM VEGETARIAN RAMEN

Tom Yum hails from Thailand. With its light, creamy texture and citrusy flavour, this dish is balanced and refreshing. You can serve this ramen on a hot summer night with a crisp, cool drink.

Prep time 25 mins   **Cook time** 40 mins   **Yield** 4 bowls

1.4l (2½ pints) **Vegetarian Stock**

4 cloves garlic, finely chopped

5cm (2in) knob galangal or ginger, sliced

2 whole stalks lemongrass, peeled and chopped in 7.5cm (3in) pieces

3 kaffir lime leaves

2 tsp Thai chilli garlic paste

1 tsp sea salt

1½ tsp sugar

2 tbsp white soy sauce

juice of 1 lime

175g (6oz) oyster mushrooms, trimmed

8 cherry tomatoes

175g (6oz) firm tofu, diced

120ml (4fl oz) coconut milk

680g (24oz) fresh **Ramen Noodles**

45g (1½oz) spring onions, finely chopped

45g (1½oz) coriander, roughly chopped

1 lime, cut into 4 wedges

1 In a large pan over a medium heat, bring the Vegetarian Stock to a simmer.

2 Add the garlic, galangal, lemongrass, and kaffir lime leaves. Cover the pan, and simmer for 30 minutes. Strain the broth, discarding the solids.

3 Bring the broth back up to a simmer and add the Thai chilli garlic paste, salt, sugar, white soy sauce, lime juice (to taste), oyster mushrooms, cherry tomatoes, tofu, and coconut milk. Simmer for 5 minutes.

4 While the broth is simmering, in a large pan of boiling water over a high heat, cook the Ramen Noodles for 50 seconds, stirring occasionally. Drain, rinse, and divide between 4 deep serving bowls.

5 Fill the bowls with the hot broth, just covering the noodles. Garnish each bowl with the spring onions and coriander, and serve with the lime wedges.

TOMATO MISO VEGETARIAN RAMEN

This ramen is as comforting as a bowl of tomato soup, but with the added depth of salty miso and the addition of delicious, chewy noodles.

Prep time 20 mins   **Cook time** 15 mins   **Yield** 4 bowls

1.4l (2½ pints) **Vegetarian Stock**

6 tomatoes, cored and peeled

1 tbsp tomato purée

1 tbsp sugar

1 tbsp white soy sauce

3 tbsp vegetarian red miso paste

2 tsp fermented chilli bean paste

680g (24oz) fresh **Ramen Noodles**

45g (1½oz) spring onions, finely chopped

1 lime, cut into 4 wedges

1 In a large pan over a medium heat, bring the Vegetarian Stock to a simmer.

2 Chop the tomatoes into bite-sized pieces, and add to the broth.

3 Add the tomato purée, sugar, and white soy sauce. Simmer for 5 minutes.

4 Add the vegetarian red miso paste and chilli bean paste. Simmer for 5 minutes.

5 While the broth is simmering, in a large pan of boiling water over a high heat, cook the Ramen Noodles for 50 seconds, stirring occasionally. Drain, rinse, and divide between 4 deep serving bowls.

6 Fill the bowls with the hot broth, just covering the noodles.

7 Garnish each bowl with the spring onions, and serve with lime wedges.

COCONUT CURRY TOFU VEGETARIAN RAMEN

Coconut milk and curry powder are a wonderful marriage of creamy and sharp flavours. Lime juice is an important addition that highlights and balances the curry. Coriander finishes this dish with a bold, fresh flavour.

Prep time 20 mins   **Cook time** 15 mins   **Yield** 4 bowls

1.4l (2½ pints) **Vegetarian Stock**

120ml (4fl oz) coconut milk

1 tsp grated ginger

1 tsp sea salt

2 tsp curry powder

8 button mushrooms, thinly sliced

1 tsp crushed chilli flakes

2½ tbsp mirin

1 tbsp white soy sauce

1 tsp sugar

175g (6oz) tofu, diced

85g (3oz) baby spinach

1½ tbsp lime juice

680g (24oz) fresh **Ramen Noodles**

4 **Marinated Soft-Boiled Eggs**, sliced in half lengthways

45g (1½oz) spring onions, finely chopped

45g (1½oz) coriander, roughly chopped

1 In a large pan over a medium heat, bring the Vegetarian Stock to a simmer.

2 Add the coconut milk, ginger, salt, curry powder, button mushrooms, crushed chilli flakes, mirin, white soy sauce, and sugar. Simmer for 5 minutes.

3 Add the tofu, baby spinach, and lime juice. Simmer for 5 minutes.

4 While the broth is simmering, in a large pan of boiling water over a high heat, cook the Ramen Noodles for 50 seconds, stirring occasionally. Drain, rinse, and divide between 4 deep serving bowls.

5 Fill the serving bowls with the hot broth, just covering the noodles.

6 Garnish each bowl with the Marinated Soft-Boiled Eggs, spring onions, and coriander.

HOW TO MAKE TOFU FROM SCRATCH

While widely considered a health food, tofu is a staple of both vegetarian and Japanese diets. You can find tofu in many different varieties: silken, soft, firm, and extra firm. Tofu is made from mature soya beans that have been dried (known as daizu), as well as nigari, which acts as a coagulant (solidifier). If you'd like fresh firm tofu to add to your Coconut Curry Tofu Vegetarian Ramen, simply follow these steps.

Prep time 13 hours **Cook time** 20 mins
Yield 400g (14oz)

200g (7oz) dried soya beans
2 tsp nigari

Special Equipment:
Food processor
Colander
Finely woven cotton cloth
Soup ladle
680g (1½lb) weight, such as a plate
   (to weigh down tofu)

1 In a large bowl filled with 1l (1¾ pints) water, soak the dried soya beans overnight, about 8–12 hours.

2 In a food processor, grind the soya beans and soaking water for 2 minutes, or until fine.

3 In a large pan over a medium heat, bring 1.2l (2 pints) water to the boil. Add the ground soya beans and stir continuously with a wooden spatula. Just before the mixture comes to the boil, reduce the heat to low and cook, stirring continuously, for 8 minutes.

4 Line a colander with finely woven cotton cloth, and place over a large pan. Strain the mixture through the cloth, and discard the solids.

5 Cook the soya milk strained into the pan over a low heat, stirring continuously with the wooden spatula. When the temperature registers between 66–68°C (150–155°F), remove the pan from the heat.

6 In a small bowl filled with 6 tablespoons lukewarm water, dissolve the nigari.

7 Add half of the nigari mixture to the soya milk, stirring with the spatula in a whirlpool pattern. While the soya milk is swirling, add the remaining nigari mixture, stirring gently afterwards in a figure-of-eight pattern. You should notice the soya milk beginning to coagulate. Cover the pan, and leave to stand for 15 minutes.

8 Line a colander with a tightly woven cotton cloth (don't reuse the previous one), and set over a bowl that can support it. With a soup ladle, gently transfer the coagulated soya milk to the cloth-lined colander.

9 Fold the cloth over top of the coagulated soya milk, and place a weight on top. Leave to stand for 15 minutes.

10 Remove the weight and gently transfer the bowl to a sink filled with cold water to cool. Once chilled, unfold the cloth, and gently lift out the finished tofu.

11 Use the tofu immediately, or store in an airtight container with fresh, cold water in the fridge for up to 1 week.

SWEETCORN CHOWDER RAMEN

Fresh sweetcorn is the star of this vegetarian ramen dish. It's enhanced by the salty, complex flavour of the miso. The addition of cream provides a lovely richness to the ramen.

Prep time 20 mins   **Cook time** 15 mins   **Yield** 4 bowls

1 tbsp vegetable oil

1l (1¾ pints) **Vegetarian Stock**

1 small onion, diced

1 clove garlic, finely chopped

500g (1lb 2oz) cooked sweetcorn kernels

500ml (16fl oz) single cream

2½ tbsp vegetarian white miso paste

2 tsp mirin

1 tsp sea salt

680g (24oz) fresh **Ramen Noodles**

4 knobs butter (about 2 tbsp)

50g (1¾oz) chives, finely chopped

Special Equipment:
Hand-held blender

1 Heat the vegetable oil in a large pan over a medium heat. Add the onion, and sauté until translucent. Add the garlic, and sauté for 1 minute, until fragrant.

2 Add the Vegetarian Stock, 350g (12oz) sweetcorn, cream, vegetarian white miso paste, mirin, and salt. Simmer for 10 minutes.

3 Using a hand-held blender, blend the broth until much of the sweetcorn has been incorporated, while still leaving some larger kernel chunks. Add the remaining sweetcorn, and simmer for 5 minutes.

4 While the broth is simmering, in a large pan of boiling water over a high heat, cook the Ramen Noodles for 50 seconds, stirring occasionally. Drain, rinse, and divide between 4 deep serving bowls.

5 Fill the bowls with the hot broth, just covering the noodles. Place 1 knob butter in the middle of each bowl, and sprinkle with the chives.

ACCOMPANiMENTS TO RAMEN

While ramen is a dish in itself, many light, tasty accompaniments can complement a bowl of ramen, such as light salads, edamame, and gyoza (Japanese dumplings).

GYOZA

Gyoza is the Japanese version of dumplings. Crisp on the bottom and steamed on top, these delicate yummies will leave you clamouring for more.

Prep time 20 mins **Cook time** 20 mins
Yield 20 gyoza

4 tbsp plus 2 tsp soy sauce

4 tbsp rice wine vinegar

1 garlic clove, finely chopped

1 tsp grated ginger

3 spring onions, green part only, finely chopped

¼ tsp crushed chilli flakes

350g (12oz) green cabbage, finely chopped

½ tsp sea salt

140g (5oz) minced pork

1 tsp ginger, finely chopped

2 tsp garlic, finely chopped

1½ tsp red miso paste

1 tsp sesame oil

1 tsp mirin

30g (1oz) cornflour

20 gyoza skins

120ml (4fl oz) warm water

2 tbsp vegetable oil

Special Equipment:
Bamboo steamer or double boiler

1 To make the dipping sauce, in a small bowl, place the 4 tablespoons soy sauce, the rice wine vinegar, garlic clove, ginger, 1 spring onion, and crushed chilli flakes. Whisk to combine. Set aside.

2 In a large bowl, mix the green cabbage and salt. Allow to sit for 15 minutes to draw the liquid out. Wrap the cabbage in a cheesecloth or thin, clean kitchen towel, and wring it out tightly.

3 Return the cabbage to a dry large bowl and add the pork, ginger, garlic, remaining spring onions, red miso paste, remaining soy sauce, sesame oil, and mirin. Mix well with your hands to combine evenly.

4 Lightly dust a baking sheet with the cornflour. Fill a small bowl with warm water. Hold one gyoza skin (flour side facing down) in your palm and pop 1 tablespoon of the pork mixture in the centre. Dip a finger in warm water, and run it along the outer edge of the gyoza skin.

5 Fold over the gyoza skin, and pinch it together, making little folds as you go. Make sure to seal it entirely. Place the finished gyoza on the floured baking sheet, spacing them out so they're not touching.

6 Spray a bamboo steamer or double boiler with non-stick cooking spray, and then place the gyoza on the surface. Steam the gyoza over a high heat until translucent, about 10–12 minutes.

7 Heat a large pan with vegetable oil over a medium-high heat. Add the steamed gyoza to the hot pan and brown on both sides, about 2–3 minutes per side. Serve with the dipping sauce.

EDAMAME

Edamame, otherwise known as soya beans, are widely available frozen in most supermarkets. Lightly boiled and salted, this healthy side dish is a perfect snack or accompaniment to a heavier dish like ramen.

Prep time 5 mins   **Cook time** 5 mins   **Yield** 450g (1lb) edamame

1.4l (2½ pints) water
450g (1lb) frozen edamame
½ tbsp sea salt

1 In a large pan over a high heat, bring the water to the boil.

2 Add the edamame, and cook for 5 minutes. Drain well.

3 Sprinkle the salt on the edamame, and toss to coat. Serve hot, cold, or at room temperature.

Edamame Serving Tips: You've probably seen edamame as an appetizer at Japanese restaurants. It's great not only as an accompaniment to ramen, but also for adding to ramen and other Japanese dishes in its hulled form.

CUCUMBER-AVOCADO SALAD WiTH CARROT-GiNGER DRESSiNG

A perfect summer salad, this dish has a healthy and delicious dressing that is sweet from the carrot and tangy from the ginger. The creamy avocado provides a nice contrast to the crunchy cucumber.

Prep time 5 mins   **Yield** 4 medium salads

2 small carrots, roughly chopped

1 tbsp shallot, finely chopped

2 tsp grated ginger

2½ tbsp rice wine vinegar

2 tbsp vegetable oil

1 tsp white miso paste (optional)

2 tbsp honey

1 tbsp water

1 head round lettuce, rinsed

2 ripe avocados, peeled, pitted, and sliced

1 large cucumber, peeled, sliced in half lengthways, seeded, and sliced

¼ tsp sea salt

Special Equipment:

Food processor

1 In the food processor, make the dressing by adding the carrots, shallot, ginger, rice wine vinegar, vegetable oil, white miso paste (if using), honey, and water. Pulse until well mixed.

2 Arrange the lettuce on 4 plates. Top the lettuce with the avocados and cucumber.

3 Sprinkle each salad with salt. Drizzle the dressing over each salad.

SHISHITO PEPPERS

One out of every 10 shishito peppers is hot (the rest are sweet and flavorsome), making eating them a culinary game of roulette! The peppers can be cooked in a variety of ways, including boiled, stir-fried, and grilled.

Prep time 5 mins   **Cook time** 15 mins   **Yield** 225g (8oz) peppers

1 tbsp extra-virgin olive oil

225g (8oz) shishito peppers

2 tsp sea salt

1 tbsp fresh lemon juice

1 tsp shichimi togarashi powder

1 Heat the olive oil in a large pan over a high heat.

2 Once the pan is very hot, but not smoking, turn down to a medium heat and add the shishito peppers.

3 Cook the peppers for 10–12 minutes, tossing them frequently and allowing the skins to blister.

4 Once cooked, sprinkle on the salt, lemon juice, and shichimi togarashi powder. Serve immediately.

Soy-Glazed Shishito Peppers: Mix 2 tablespoons soy sauce, 2 teaspoons honey, 1 tablespoon lemon juice, 1 teaspoon finely chopped ginger, and 1 teaspoon finely chopped garlic. Whisk to combine. Add to peppers after they have been cooking for 5 minutes.

AVOCADO SALAD

Light, fresh, and delicious, this salad is the perfect accompaniment to a hot bowl of ramen. The tangy ginger-vinegar dressing provides a lovely contrast to the mild avocado.

Prep time 4 mins   **Yield** 4 medium salads

1 tbsp vegetable oil

1 tsp sesame oil

2 tbsp rice wine vinegar

2 tbsp mirin

1 tsp grated ginger

1 tsp sugar

250–500g (9oz–1lb 2oz) salad leaves

2 ripe avocados, peeled, pitted, and sliced in half

2 tbsp toasted sesame seeds

1 In a small bowl, place the vegetable oil, sesame oil, rice wine vinegar, mirin, ginger, and sugar. Whisk to combine.

2 In a large bowl, toss the salad leaves with the dressing. Arrange on 4 plates.

3 Neatly fan the avocado slices on each salad plate.

4 Sprinkle each salad with the toasted sesame seeds.

SPiCY BEAN SPROUT SALAD

Simple, crunchy, and spicy, this bean salad has a kick from shichimi togarashi powder, the Japanese seven-spice blend.

Prep time 5 mins **Cook time** 2 mins
Yield 4 small plates

250g (9oz) bean sprouts

1 tbsp sesame oil

1 tbsp vegetable oil

2 tsp soy sauce

1 tsp shichimi togarashi powder

¼ tsp sea salt

45g (1½oz) spring onion greens, finely chopped

2 tbsp toasted sesame seeds

About Bean Sprouts: Bean sprouts are a common ingredient in Asian cooking. They are often used in stir-fries and soups, and as a garnish. Plus, sprouted beans require little cooking time.

1 In a large pan over a high heat, bring 1.4l (2½ pints) water to the boil.

2 Add the bean sprouts, and cook for 1–2 minutes. Drain in a colander, and rinse with cold water. Set aside.

3 In a medium bowl, combine the sesame oil, vegetable oil, soy sauce, shichimi togarashi powder, and salt. Whisk well.

4 Add the bean sprouts, and toss to coat evenly. Divide between 4 small salad plates.

5 Garnish with the spring onions and toasted sesame seeds.

RECIPES FOR TRANSFORMING INSTANT RAMEN

If you recall, instant ramen noodles are dried or precooked noodles that are usually eaten after being cooked in boiling water for a few minutes. These noodles are typically sold with a packet of flavouring, such as beef or chicken. While instant ramen has a reputation as cheap fare for students, these noodles can provide a quick, easy way to put together a meal in no time.

IMPROVING PACKAGED NOODLES

By simply adding some seasonings and toppings, you can alter the taste of instant noodles to something more flavoursome and exotic.

Miso paste, chilli garlic sauce, curry powder, vinegar, white pepper, crushed chilli flakes, and oils can add some unique flavours to packaged noodles. The ramen can then be topped with quick-cooking vegetables, eggs, or even cured meat (such as bacon or ham) for a full and pleasant taste sensation.

NEW USES FOR NOODLES AND FLAVOURING

The noodles and flavour packets don't even have to be the base of a recipe. You can also do endlessly interesting things to transform their ingredients into completely different dishes!

For instance, uncooked ramen noodles can be used as a crunchy topping on salads. And recently, intrepid chefs have discarded the noodles and simply used the flavour packet to season their dishes.

From ramen noodle burger buns, to cold salads, to more sophisticated egg dishes, instant ramen is versatile and downright fun to play with.

A NOTE ABOUT THE RECIPES

These recipes use the little blocks of instant noodles with the seasoning packaged in a separate envelope, not the type sold in foam cups. If you're worried about the high salt content that can come from using instant noodles, you can simply discard the flavouring packet.

ASiAN RAMEN NOODLE COLESLAW SALAD

Instant ramen noodles are a great addition to a cold salad. The honey and mango give this salad a touch of sweetness, which is balanced by the tart and sour flavours of the rice wine vinegar and lime juice.

Prep time 20 mins   **Yield** 350–450g (12oz–1lb)

160ml (6fl oz) vegetable oil

1 tsp sesame oil

90ml (3fl oz) honey

80ml (2½fl oz) rice wine vinegar

3 tbsp soy sauce

1 tsp Thai chilli garlic sauce

1 tbsp lime juice

¾ tsp sea salt

¼ tsp freshly ground black pepper

2 x 85g (3oz) pack instant ramen noodles (discard flavour packets)

125g (4½oz) shredded carrots

125g (4½oz) shredded green or red cabbage

1 ripe avocado, peeled, pitted, and diced

1 mango, peeled, pitted, and diced

75g (2½oz) roasted cashews

5 spring onions, finely chopped

1 In a small bowl, whisk the vegetable oil, sesame oil, honey, rice wine vinegar, soy sauce, Thai chilli garlic sauce, lime juice, salt, and black pepper. Set aside

2 Crumble the uncooked instant ramen noodles into a large bowl. Add the carrots, green cabbage, avocado, mango, cashews, and spring onions.

3 Cover in the dressing and toss well to combine all of the ingredients.

RAMEN BURGERS

The noodle buns of ramen burgers are crispy on the outside and soft on the inside, and there's a reason they have such a cult following! They're easy to make and utterly delicious, with a spicy ketchup that includes Thai chilli garlic sauce.

Prep time 30 mins   **Cook time** 15 mins   **Yield** 4 burgers

3 x 85g (3oz) pack instant ramen noodles (discard flavour packets)

2 eggs

1 tsp sea salt

½ tsp freshly ground black pepper

450g (1lb) minced beef

1 tbsp soy sauce

1 tsp sesame oil

1 tbsp plus 90ml (3fl oz) ketchup

4 slices Cheddar cheese

2 tbsp vegetable oil

1 tbsp Thai chilli garlic sauce

4 lettuce leaves, any type (optional)

Special Equipment:

8 ramekins (the size you would like your burgers to be)

1 Boil a large pan of water over a high heat. Add the instant ramen noodles and cook until tender, about 3 minutes.

2 Rinse the noodles under cold water, drain well, and set aside. Beat the eggs in a bowl. Season with the salt and black pepper. Add the noodles and stir well to combine.

3 Divide the egg mixture between 8 ramekins, squeezing out excess egg. Top each ramekin with cling film, pressing down so the film touches the noodles. Refrigerate for at least 20 minutes.

4 In a medium bowl, mix the beef, soy sauce, sesame oil, and 1 tablespoon ketchup. Divide into 4 patties. In a large frying pan on a medium heat, cook the patties for 2–3 minutes each side, until the desired doneness. After flipping the burgers to the second side, top each with 1 slice Cheddar cheese. When cooked, set aside.

5 In the same pan, heat the vegetable oil on a medium heat. Carefully remove the noodles from the ramekins, and fry for 3 minutes on each side, until golden.

6 In a small bowl, mix the remaining ketchup and Thai chilli garlic sauce.

7 Build your burger! Put 1 ramen bun on each of the 4 plates; top with a burger patty, spicy ketchup, and lettuce; and place another ramen bun on top.

RAMEN FRITTATA

Frittatas are a fantastic breakfast dish and can be made with a variety of your favourite ingredients. The noodles help give the frittata extra structure and a chewy consistency. The flavour packets season the egg mixture, eliminating the need for additional salt and pepper.

Prep time 10 mins   **Cook time** 20 mins   **Yield** 1 large frittata

3 x 85g (3oz) pack chicken-flavoured instant ramen noodles

8 eggs

1 tbsp butter

85g (3oz) button mushrooms, sliced

85g (3oz) chopped ham

45g (1½oz) grated Cheddar cheese

Special Equipment:

Large ovenproof sauté pan

1 Preheat the oven to 175°C (375°F). Boil a large pan of water over a high heat. Cook the instant ramen noodles for 3 minutes, until tender. Strain, rinse under cold water, and drain well.

2 In a medium bowl, whisk together the eggs and ramen packet flavourings. Add the noodles, and stir to combine.

3 In a large ovenproof frying pan over a medium-high heat, melt the butter. Add the button mushrooms, and cook for 3–4 minutes. Add the ham, and stir to heat through, about 1–2 minutes.

4 Pour the egg-noodle mixture into the pan, and stir with a rubber spatula.

5 Once the egg mixture starts to set, sprinkle the cheese on top, and pop in the oven for 6–8 minutes, until the frittata is puffed and golden. Cut into quarters and serve immediately.

GLOSSARY

al dente   Italian for "against the teeth"; refers to cooked pasta or rice that's still slightly firm.

assari   A light ramen broth.

bake   To cook in a dry oven.

baking powder   A dry ingredient used to increase volume and lighten or leaven baked goods.

baste   To keep foods moist during cooking by applying a liquid.

beat   To quickly mix substances.

beech mushroom   Named after the trees they grow on, these mushrooms have a bitter taste that can be eliminated with cooking. Once cooked, the mushrooms have a nutty flavour and crunchy texture.

blanch   To place a food in boiling water for about 1 minute or less to partially cook and then douse with cool water to halt the cooking.

blend   To completely mix something, usually with a blender or food processor, slower than beating.

boil   To heat a liquid to the point water turns into steam, causing the liquid to bubble. Also, to cook food in boiling water.

bonito flakes   Fish flakes used for dashi stock, made from skipjack tuna.

bouillon   Dried essence of stock from chicken, beef, vegetables, or other ingredients. It's popular as a starting ingredient for soups.

braise   To cook with the introduction of a liquid, usually over a period of time.

brine   A highly salted, often seasoned liquid used to flavour and preserve foods. Also, to soak or preserve a food by submerging it in brine.

broth   A stock that has been seasoned and flavoured.

brown   To cook in a frying pan, turning, until the food's surface is seared and brown in colour, to lock in the juices.

caramelize   To cook vegetables or meat in butter or oil over a low heat until they soften, sweeten, and develop a caramel colour. Also, to cook sugar over a low heat until it develops a sweet caramel flavour.

cayenne pepper   A fiery spice made from hot chilli peppers, especially the slender, red, very hot cayenne.

chashu   Braised pork loin or pork belly used as a topping for ramen.

chilli (or chillie)   A term for a number of hot peppers, ranging from the relatively mild ancho to the blisteringly hot habanero.

chilli garlic sauce   Also known as sambal, a pungent, spicy condiment widely used in Asia.

chilli powder   A warm, rich seasoning blend that includes chilli pepper, cumin, garlic, and oregano.

Chinese black vinegar   An aged vinegar with a rich, woody, fruity flavour.

Chinese five-spice powder   A pungent mixture of cinnamon, cloves, fennel seed, anise, and Szechuan peppercorns.

Chinese sausage   A broad term for sausages made in China, the most popular being a thin, sweet, dried sausage.

chive   A herb that grows in bunches of long leaves and offers a light onion flavour.

chop   To cut into pieces, usually qualified such as "coarsely chopped" or with a size measurement such as "chopped into 1.25cm (½in) pieces." "Finely chopped" is much closer to minced.

cider vinegar   A vinegar produced from apple cider, popular in North America.

coconut milk   A non-dairy liquid made from grated coconut and water.

coriander   A member of the parsley family used in Mexican dishes (especially salsa) and some Asian dishes. The seed of the **coriander** plant is the spice coriander.

coriander seed   A rich, warm, spicy seed used in all types of recipes.

cornflour   A thickener made from the refined starch of a corn kernel's endosperm. Before it's added to a recipe, it's often mixed with a liquid to make a paste and to avoid clumps.

cumin   A fiery, smoky-tasting spice most often used ground in Middle Eastern and Indian dishes.

curry   Rich, spicy, Indian-style sauces and the dishes prepared with them. Curry powder is the base seasoning.

curry powder   A blend of rich and flavoursome spices such as hot pepper, nutmeg, cumin, cinnamon, pepper, and turmeric.

dash   A few drops, usually of a liquid, released by a quick shake.

dashi   A Japanese stock made from kelp and bonito flakes that's used as a base in many dishes.

deglaze   To scrape up bits of meat and seasonings left in a pan after cooking, usually by adding a liquid such as wine or broth, to create a flavoursome stock.

devein   To remove the dark vein from the back of a large prawn with a sharp knife.

dice   To cut into small cubes about 5mm (¼in) square.

Dijon mustard   A hearty, spicy mustard made in the style of the Dijon region of France.

double boiler   A set of two nesting pans that provide consistent, moist heat. The bottom pan holds a shallow amount of water, and the top pan holds the food.

dredge   To coat a piece of food on all sides with a dry substance such as flour or polenta.

edamame   Fresh, plump, green soya beans often served steamed and either shelled or still in the pod.

emulsion   A combination of liquid ingredients that don't normally mix well (such as a fat or oil with water) that are beaten together to create a thick liquid. Creating emulsions must be done carefully and rapidly to ensure the particles of one ingredient are suspended in the other.

enoki mushroom   Tiny and thin mushrooms, with a small cap. Wild versions can be found in a variety of colours and shapes, while cultivated enoki are bright white and long-stemmed. These mushrooms are mild and sweet in flavour, and rich in antioxidants.

finely chop   To cut into very small pieces, smaller than diced, about 3mm (⅛ in) or smaller.

flour   Grains ground into a meal. Wheat is the most common flour, but oats, rye, buckwheat, soya beans, chickpeas, and others are also used. *See also* plain flour.

fold   To combine a dense and a light mixture with a gentle move from the middle of the bowl outwards to preserve the mixture's airy nature.

fry   *See* sauté.

galangal   A root native to Southeast Asia that's similar in flavour to ginger but more pungent.

garlic   A member of the onion family, a pungent and flavoursome vegetable used in many savoury dishes. A garlic bulb contains multiple cloves; each clove, when chopped, yields about 1 teaspoon garlic.

ginger   A flavoursome root available fresh or dried and ground that adds a pungent, sweet, and spicy quality to a dish.

grill   To cook in a dry oven under the overhead high-heat element.

gyoza   A Japanese dumpling, similar to Chinese dumplings, usually made with pork and cabbage.

hen-of-the-woods   A bold-flavoured mushroom that resembles the ruffled feathers of a chicken.

hoisin sauce   A sweet Asian condiment similar to ketchup made with soya beans, sesame, chilli peppers, and sugar.

infusion   A liquid in which flavoursome ingredients such as herbs have been steeped to extract their flavour into the liquid.

julienne   A French word meaning "to slice into very thin pieces".

kansui   An alkaline water used to make ramen noodles. Kansui gives the noodles their firm, chewy texture and yellow colour.

kelp   Edible seaweed widely eaten in parts of Asia and used to make dashi stock.

knead   To work dough, often with your hands, to make it pliable so it holds gas bubbles as it bakes.

kotteri   A rich, thick style of ramen.

marinate   To soak a food in a seasoned sauce to impart flavour and make tender, as with meat.

marsala wine   An Italian fortified wine, available either dry or sweet.

matsutake   A thick and meaty mushroom that can be white or brown. Hard to find and highly prized, matsutakes have a unique, spicy aroma.

menma   A Japanese fermented bamboo condiment use to top noodle soups.

mirin   A rice wine used extensively in Japanese cooking.

mise en place   A French term that refers to the preparation of equipment and food before a meal begins.

miso   A flavoursome fermented soya bean paste, key in many Japanese dishes.

miso ramen   A type of ramen made with miso.

narutomaki   A Japanese fish cake with a pink spiral in the middle.

nori   An edible seaweed.

oyster mushroom   With a smooth cap that can grow up to 20cm (8in) wide and closely resembles an oyster, this mushroom grows in layers. Subtle in flavour and very versatile, oyster mushrooms tend to soak up the flavour of whatever they are cooked with and have a soft texture.

pak choi   A member of the cabbage family with thick stems, crisp texture, and fresh flavour.

parsley   A fresh-tasting green leafy herb, often used as a garnish.

pinch   An unscientific measurement for the amount of an ingredient you can hold between your finger and thumb.

plain flour   Flour that contains only the inner part of the wheat grain.

portobello mushroom   A large, brown, chewy, flavoursome mushroom.

preheat   To turn on an oven, grill, or other cooking appliance early so it will be at the desired temperature when the dish is ready to be cooked.

radish   A root crop with a pungent, sweet flavour.

reduce   To boil or simmer a broth or sauce to remove some of the water content and yield a more concentrated flavour.

reserve   To hold a specified ingredient for use later in a recipe.

rice wine vinegar   A mild, sweet vinegar made from rice wine.

roast To cook food uncovered in an oven, usually without additional liquid.

rocket A spicy-peppery salad leaf that has a sharp, distinctive flavour.

sage A herb with a slightly musty, fruity, lemon-rind scent and a "sunny" flavour.

sauté To pan-cook over lower heat than is used for frying.

scant An ingredient measurement directive not to add any extra, perhaps even leaving the measurement a tad short.

sea salt A coarse-grained salt made without additives or iodine.

sear To quickly brown the exterior of a food, especially meat, over high heat.

sesame oil An oil made from pressing sesame seeds. It's tasteless if clear and aromatic and flavoursome if brown.

shallot A member of the onion family that grows in a bulb somewhat like garlic but has a milder onion flavour.

shellfish A broad range of seafood, including clams, mussels, oysters, crabs, prawns, and lobster.

shichimi togarashi powder A Japanese condiment with a variety of spices such as pepper, ginger, seaweed, chilli, sesame, and orange peel.

shiitake A large, dark brown mushroom with a hearty, meaty flavour.

shio ramen A ramen made with a salt base.

shoyu ramen A ramen made with a soy sauce base.

simmer To boil gently so the liquid barely bubbles.

skillet (also frying pan) A flat-bottomed metal pan with a handle designed to cook food on a hob.

skim To remove fat or other material from the top of a liquid.

soft-boiled egg A cooked egg with a runny yolk and solid white used to top ramen.

soya milk Plant milk made with soya beans.

spring onion A mild onion with a long green stem, also called green onion and, in the US, scallion.

steam To suspend a food over boiling water and allow the heat of the steam to cook the food.

steep To let something sit in hot water, as in steeping tea in hot water.

stir-fry   To cook small pieces of food in a wok or frying pan over a high heat, moving and turning the food quickly to cook all sides.

stock   A flavoursome liquid made by cooking meats, fish, and/or vegetables until the liquid absorbs these flavours. The stock is strained, and the solids are discarded. Stock can be eaten alone or used as a base for soups, stews, and so on.

tahini   A paste made from sesame seeds used to flavour many Middle Eastern dishes.

tamarind   A sweet, pungent, flavoursome fruit used in Indian-style sauces and curries.

tempeh   An Indonesian food made by culturing and fermenting soya beans into a cake. It's high in protein and fibre.

teriyaki   A Japanese-style sauce made of soy sauce, rice wine, ginger, and sugar.

tofu   A cheese-like substance made from soya beans and soya milk.

tonkotsu   A thick ramen base made from pork bones that's simmered for a long time.

tsukemen   A type of ramen where the broth and noodles are served separately, with the noodles usually at room temperature or cold.

turmic   A spicy, pungent yellow root. It's the source of the yellow colour in many prepared mustards.

umami   The fifth taste after salty, sweet, sour, and bitter. Umami is described as a meaty, rich, and full flavour.

vegetable steamer   A perforated insert designed to fit in or on a saucepan to hold food to be steamed above boiling water.

vinegar   An acidic liquid often made from fermented grapes, apples, or rice and used as a dressing and seasoning. *See also* Chinese black vinegar; cider vinegar; rice wine vinegar; wine vinegar.

wakame   Thin seaweed strips used as a ramen topping.

whisk   To rapidly mix, introducing air to the mixture.

white soy sauce   A thin, clear soy sauce with a delicate flavour. It's produced in a much smaller quantity than dark soy sauce.

wine vinegar   Vinegar produced from red or white wine.

wood ear   A mushroom that resembles an ear, wrinkled and floppy in appearance. These are typically used because of their crisp texture rather than their taste.

zest   Small slivers of peel, usually from citrus fruit such as a lemon, lime, or orange.

iNDEX

ABOUT THE AUTHOR

NELL BENTON owns The National Café, located in the Walker's Point neighborhood in Milwaukee, Wisconsin USA. The café, which she purchased in 2010, specializes in fresh, locally sourced dishes with an international flair. Born to a British mother and American father, Nell grew up in Los Angeles, California, and Green Bay, Wisconsin, with frequent trips to visit relatives in Devon, England. Her formative years were spent following her mother and grandmother around the garden and kitchen.

After collecting a degree in anthropology/sociology at St. Norbert College in De Pere, Wisconsin, Nell spent almost a decade living and working all over the world, which fuelled her passion for international cuisine. After stints in Indonesia, Egypt, and England, Nell obtained a culinary degree from The Art Institute of Fort Lauderdale, Florida. She travels often to Asia to further her knowledge of Asian cuisine.

ACKNOWLEDGMENTS

I can't sufficiently express my deep gratitude to my hardworking, over-educated, kind-hearted café staff for their unwavering support and willingness to take over many of my duties, allowing me to focus on this book: Angela Wierzbinski, my manager; Meg Shecterle, my assistant manager; Arielle Yanasak, my catering manager; Julia Borden, my beverage manager; Victor Hernandez; Mandi Hollis; Dan Bernath; and Ashley Parrill. Thank you for helping me love what I do!

To my friend and chief recipe tester, Chef Thi Cao: thank you for the endless hours in the kitchen helping me test recipes, play with flavours, and roll out noodles. There's no one I love cooking with more.

A huge thank you to Michael and Shelly Diedrick. Without their generosity and kindness, I wouldn't have my café.

A heartfelt thank you to my editor, Nathalie Mornu, for her time, expertise, and patience in going through each page of the book with me.

There are many people who have helped me along my culinary journey and given me a hand in getting my business off the ground. Scott and Marjorie Moon, Clare Norton, Tom Crofts, Nigel LeQuesne, Chef Kevin Guay, Barbara Benton, David Turnpaugh, Andrew Bruce, Sean Henninger, Gary and Denise Wierzbinski, Joe Sutter,

Amanda Joy, and Jax: without your support, I would not be where I am today. My heartfelt thanks.

Finally, to my amazing family, thank you for everything. To Mary Maloney, my twin sister and other half, for her steadfast support and encouragement; Robert Maloney, my amazing and inspiring brother; Anna Benton, my older and wiser sister; my nieces, Violet and Helena, for making me laugh and recognize the importance of play; and my parents, Jim and Helen Benton, who have filled my life with their grace, love, encouragement, and support. Thank you!

Alpha Books and DK would like to thank the following people for their hard work and dedication in making this book: Ronnie Andren, photography assistant; Kanisorn Sinprasert and Carolyne Hilario, food styling assistants; Ruthy Kirwan, recipe tester; Dave King, additional photography; and Lucy-Ruth Hathaway, additional food styling.

The publisher would like to thank the following for their kind permission to reproduce their photographs:
22-23 iStockphoto.com: Illustrious (map)
All other images © Dorling Kindersley
For further information see: www.dkimages.com